Entrepreneurship Education

The discussion around whether entrepreneurship can be taught is becoming obsolete as the number of entrepreneurship courses, specializations and degrees is rising at an unprecedented rate all over the world and the demand for entrepreneurial education teachers or instructors is constantly growing. The global community of entrepreneurial education proponents is enthusiastic about the possibility of spreading the idea of entrepreneurship, as it is believed to benefit societies and economies in addition to influencing human development on an individual level. The fervour is nurtured by public policies and the development of an enterprising culture in the public discourse. In this discourse, entrepreneurship is treated as a panacea for numerous social and economic problems.

This book is a solid reference point for all those who are interested in conducting research on entrepreneurial education or engaged in teaching entrepreneurship. It is a compendium of knowledge about entrepreneurial education as a research field, seen from the perspective of the last four decades, its complete contemporary history. It reviews the progress of the field from the outset to the present in terms of its socio-economic context, changes in the academic community, as well as its research focus and methodological development. This uniquely comprehensive book is a resource for both knowledge on entrepreneurial education research and inspiration for future studies within the field.

This timely and relevant book provides practical insights for educators when developing their teaching practice and will be of interest to entrepreneurship educators and entrepreneurship education researchers.

Gustav Hägg is Researcher at Sten K. Johnson Centre for Entrepreneurship, Lund University, and Assistant Professor at Malmö University, Sweden.

Agnieszka Kurczewska is Associate Professor at the Faculty of Economics and Sociology at the University of Lodz, Poland.

Routledge Focus on Business and Management

The fields of business and management have grown exponentially as areas of research and education. This growth presents challenges for readers trying to keep up with the latest important insights. *Routledge Focus on Business and Management* presents small books on big topics and how they intersect with the world of business research.

Individually, each title in the series provides coverage of a key academic topic, whilst collectively, the series forms a comprehensive collection across the business disciplines.

Crony Capitalism in US Health Care
Anatomy of a Dysfunctional System
Naresh Khatri

Entrepreneurship Education
Scholarly Progress and Future Challenges
Gustav Hägg and Agnieszka Kurczewska

Culture and Resilience at Work
A Study of Stress and Hardiness among Indian Corporate Professionals
Pallabi Mund

Optimal Spending on Cybersecurity Measures
Risk Management
Tara Kissoon

For more information about this series, please visit: www.routledge.com/Routledge-Focus-on-Business-and-Management/book-series/FBM

Entrepreneurship Education
Scholarly Progress and
Future Challenges

**Gustav Hägg and
Agnieszka Kurczewska**

Routledge
Taylor & Francis Group

NEW YORK AND LONDON

First published 2022
by Routledge
605 Third Avenue, New York, NY 10158

and by Routledge
2 Park Square, Milton Park, Abingdon, Oxon OX14 4RN

Routledge is an imprint of the Taylor & Francis Group, an informa business

© 2022 Gustav Hägg and Agnieszka Kurczewska

Library of Congress Cataloging-in-Publication Data
Names: Hägg, Gustav, 1983– author. | Kurczewska, Agnieszka, 1980– author.
Title: Entrepreneurship education : scholarly progress and future
challenges / Gustav Hägg and Agnieszka Kurczewska.
Description: New York, NY : Routledge, 2022 |
Series: Routledge focus on business and management |
Includes bibliographical references and index.
Identifiers: LCCN 2021014130 (print) | LCCN 2021014131 (ebook) |
ISBN 9781032048758 (hbk) | ISBN 9781032048765 (pbk) |
ISBN 9781003194972 (ebook)
Subjects: LCSH: Entrepreneurship. | Entrepreneurship–Study and teaching.
Classification: LCC HB615 .H2333 2022 (print) |
LCC HB615 (ebook) | DDC 658.0071–dc23
LC record available at https://lccn.loc.gov/2021014130
LC ebook record available at https://lccn.loc.gov/2021014131

ISBN: 978-1-032-04875-8 (hbk)
ISBN: 978-1-032-04876-5 (pbk)
ISBN: 978-1-003-19497-2 (ebk)

DOI: 10.4324/9781003194972

Typeset in Times New Roman
by Newgen Publishing UK

Contents

Illustrations

Figures

Tables

About the Authors

Gustav Hägg is a researcher at Sten K. Johnson Centre for Entrepreneurship, Lund University, and is currently an assistant professor at Malmö University with a PhD in entrepreneurship education and entrepreneurial learning focused on how reflective thinking can become more integrated in the learning process of student entrepreneurs. His research interests include theorizing learning in entrepreneurship education and the post-entrepreneurship education career of graduates through alumni research. He also has general interest for entrepreneurial decision making and the role of ethics in relation to entrepreneurship within the gig economy.

Agnieszka Kurczewska is a researcher in the field of entrepreneurship and entrepreneurial education. She holds a PhD in economics and is currently an associate professor at the University of Lodz in Poland, where she is also vice-rector with responsibility for external relations. She is a member of the Board of Directors of the European Council for Small Business & Entrepreneurship. Her research interests include entrepreneurship education, in particular experience-based learning, but also ethical side of entrepreneurial processes.

Introduction

The discussion on whether or not entrepreneurship can be taught is becoming obsolete. The number of entrepreneurship courses, specializations and degrees is rising at an unprecedented rate all over the world and the demand for entrepreneurial education teachers or instructors is constantly growing. The global community of entrepreneurial education[1] proponents is very enthusiastic about the possibility of spreading the idea of entrepreneurship, as it is believed to benefit societies and economies in addition to influencing human development on an individual level. Furthermore, the enthusiasm is nurtured by public policies and the development of an enterprising culture in the public discourse. In this discourse, entrepreneurship is treated as a panacea for numerous social and economic problems. The public rhetoric of entrepreneurship has affected Higher Education Institutions (HEI). The positive impact of entrepreneurship is growing exponentially (see Katz, 2008; Morris & Liguori, 2016) and can be seen in many places where teaching and learning seek to develop more entrepreneurs as well as more entrepreneurially thinking individuals. Unquestionably, in the first two decades of the 21st century, entrepreneurial education has enjoyed a prosperous period in academia. It has seen tremendous growth as a research field and there is widespread exposure to entrepreneurial education and training among citizens at all levels.

The general positive attitude towards teaching entrepreneurship set the scene for entrepreneurial education to emerge and develop as a research field. However, the academic legitimization process takes time and involves several challenges. The field is young and still fragmented

---

1 We are using entrepreneurial education as a composite term that includes both entrepreneurship and enterprising education, following the argument from Erkkilä (2000) as well as from Hägg and Gabrielsson (2019) as the two terms oftentimes occur intertwined in research discussions.

(Hägg & Gabrielsson, 2019; Nabi, Liñán, Fayolle, Krueger, & Walmsley, 2017). Accumulation of knowledge related to how and what to teach requires scientific rigour and research grounding (see Fayolle, 2013). However, development of entrepreneurial education is evolutionary, not straight forward and over the decades the heterogeneity of the phenomenon has both drawn researchers into the field as well as created largely different perspectives on what entrepreneurial education actually should lead towards (Erkkilä, 2000; Jones, 2019; Neck & Corbett, 2018). A main issue to address is whether the theoretical advancement of entrepreneurship is sufficient to create the foundations for teaching and learning. To respond to these overarching trends we build on the rigour and relevance discussion laid forward in mainstream entrepreneurship research (Fayolle, Landstrom, Gartner, & Berglund, 2016; Frank & Landström, 2016), as well as the ongoing call for legitimacy and methodological rigour in entrepreneurial education literature (Fayolle, Verzat, & Wapshott, 2016; Foliard, Pontois, Fayolle, & Diermann, 2018; Rideout & Gray, 2013) by asking the following questions:

1. What developmental trends can we see regarding theoretical and methodological advancement in studies on entrepreneurship and enterprising education?
2. What trends can be seen in the development of entrepreneurship and enterprising education in regard to contextual lenses related to the community development?

Responding to these issues would enable the setting of the boundaries of entrepreneurial education research, or at least point to the weaknesses that might exist given the criticism of little maturity and low methodological rigour, as well as limited contextual reach (Blenker, Elmholdt, Frederiksen, Korsgaard, & Wagner, 2014; Fayolle et al., 2016; Rideout & Gray, 2013).

An interesting but not entirely positive fact about entrepreneurial education is that it was initially widely conducted (mainly through experimentation based on intuition and observation of entrepreneurs) before the field actually emerged on the research map. The need for entrepreneurial education mainly derived from the grass-root demand for this type of education, not because the development of entrepreneurship as a field was scientifically adequate to be applied in teaching. The consequences are that both the field and practice were developed in an unstructured and spontaneous way. Therefore, the general picture of the field might appear somewhat blurred and thus more studies evaluating its maturity are required.

A problem that may limit the adequate development of the field is that the majority of scholars conducting studies in entrepreneurial education are its greatest supporters and often conduct empirical studies only on their own students (Rideout & Gray, 2013), where context becomes the driving force for the uniqueness of the specific study. This may influence the way in which they interpret the research findings and formulate implications for teaching practice. In such a situation, the progress of the field might be slower than expected and the research findings difficult to place in a larger context to move the knowledge base forward.

It should be noted that from the outset, entrepreneurial education has been viewed as an alternative and progressive field when compared to other sub-fields in education. In general, entrepreneurial education scholars agree that traditional pedagogy alone is not sufficient to trigger entrepreneurial thinking and acting. Consequently, there is an open call for more innovative teaching methods that can facilitate and enhance the entrepreneurial learning process. Traditional methods and approaches are considered unsuitable for the entrepreneurial context (Neck & Corbett, 2018), which is characterized by high complexity and uncertainty. This assumption is not wrong *per se*; however, it cannot be the reason for ignoring the vast scientific output that the field of education has developed throughout the past decades and even centuries. The tendency to criticize general educational theories and create *ad hoc* frameworks explaining a particular teaching intervention or form of entrepreneurial learning in a very narrow context might lead to a deadlock in terms of research in the long term. Of course entrepreneurial education has its own specific characteristics, which is why it aspires to become a field with full scientific legitimization. However, shortcut solutions without a deeper understanding of the educative processes hinder its development and call into question the reliability of its research.

Although it may sound quite provocative, the current worldwide promotion of entrepreneurial education occurs in circumstances where there is a lack of sufficient sound, research-based proof of its value and effectiveness. It is still a young field that gained its promotion and acceptability from the hand of policy, but for long-term survival and acceptance entrepreneurial education needs to focus more on knowledge accumulation and advancing its scientific foundations. The question is how can entrepreneurial education as a research field be advanced? In order to answer this, it is necessary to first discuss some of its deficiencies. We identified four, which seem to be the most prevalent.

The first deficiency can be called a terminology crisis, as it consists of misuse of basic terms from the education field and lack of sufficient theorization around them (Pittaway & Cope, 2007). For example, although a number of studies in entrepreneurial education address andragogy (how adults learn) and pedagogy (how to teach children and adolescents) and the discussion and depth is slowly developing, the underlying assumptions are in need of more scrutiny and therefore limit the understanding of these terms (Hägg & Kurczewska, 2019). The problem is that entrepreneurship terminology is not essentially the same in all studies; therefore, its usage often requires additional effort on the part of the entrepreneurial education scholar.

The second deficiency is the lack of proper use of philosophical foundations for building entrepreneurial education. The structure of scientific knowledge requires a philosophical foundation, including methodological principles and scientific reasoning, to explain and interpret reality. Although entrepreneurial education has expanded rapidly as a result of policy, its theoretical and philosophical foundation has been addressed only briefly (Fayolle, 2013; Jones, 2006; Kyrö, 2015). Less attention has been paid to the legacy of education and philosophy and its potential to make entrepreneurial learning possible (Jones, 2019; Neck & Corbett, 2018). An example could be the idea of learning entrepreneurship through experience, which is commonly used in the practice of entrepreneurial education but has not been developed with reference to the broad knowledge on experience offered by philosophy and the general educational field (see Hägg & Kurczewska, 2020). One of the reasons for this could be the fact that entrepreneurial education was developed through empirical studies on how actual entrepreneurs learn, from which entrepreneurship courses and curriculums were established.

The third deficiency is a methodological weakness demonstrated by an insufficient number of longitudinal studies measuring long-term effects of entrepreneurial education, poor replicability of studies and their weak representativeness. In addition to the above-mentioned problem of the potential bias involved in conducting studies on small groups of one's own students, the problem of the performativity of entrepreneurial education emerges. The frameworks or models used by entrepreneurial teachers and instructors during teaching affect the phenomena they purport to study and in this sense there is a risk of demonstrating that reality is more in line with theory than it really is.

The methodological challenges are linked with the fourth deficiency of entrepreneurial education as a field, which is context dependency. The problem here is that the field develops from lessons learned from single cases or contexts. Entrepreneurial education appears in very diverse contexts that are impossible to compare as the context determines the outcomes of the educational process and the general judgment of the learning process. Hence, context needs to be acknowledged when making claims on what is learnt, as otherwise it becomes impossible to tease out what could be retained when contextual influences are eliminated.

How can this book be helpful in overcoming these four deficiencies? It is supportive in the sense that it does not only systematically review and document the development of the field, but also identifies its major weaknesses and challenges. On the basis of the unique data collected based on a systematic literature review methodology of papers related to entrepreneurial education published between January 1980 and December 2018, it seeks to illustrate what has been done in entrepreneurial education so far; thus, it indicates potential areas that need increased research attention and more carefully conducted studies. The repository created consists of 447 papers, each classified after inspecting its contents by means of codes. Therefore, the book serves as a uniquely comprehensive source of both knowledge on entrepreneurial education research and inspiration for future studies to be conducted within the field, thus opening up new scholarship opportunities within the discipline.

The idea behind the book is not to critique for the sake of critiquing the progress that has been made, but to highlight the less developed areas of entrepreneurial education in order to present a realistic picture of its scientific output aimed at indicating how to move forward towards scientific excellence in research. It is only by looking backwards and synthesizing what has been done that we can make sense of how to move forward. With this book, we aim to develop useful arguments for demonstrating the growing maturity of the field and highlighting the research areas worth exploring and further advancing. We aim to interpret and understand the characteristics and evolution of entrepreneurial education research. After four decades, we are in a position to formulate meaningful conclusions about the progress of the field, as well as identify its main challenges and potential future directions. To achieve that, a critical approach needs to be applied. The book illustrates the legitimization process of entrepreneurial education research and critically assesses its progress as an academic field. It departs from the history of entrepreneurial education research and synthesizes its achievements as a field by reviewing the learning theories and teaching methods used and highlighting the importance of context. Descriptive examination of the status of entrepreneurial education sets the scene for a more thorough and systematic analysis of long-term trends in the field.

The most important phenomenon we aim to illustrate in this book is the development of entrepreneurial education as a scholarly field. Each field presents its own characteristics in terms of growth patterns, progress in theoretical developments and methodological choices, or even the research community that is formed around it (Landström, 2020). Our goal is to outline how the field has evolved from its emergence until the present. By treating the development of the field as a process, we seek to better understand how the field performs over time in order to synthesize its development.

The structure of the book is as follows. It consists of four chapters. The first chapter is a brief history of the field with focus on the socio-economic background of the rise of entrepreneurial education and its path towards academic legitimization. The second chapter presents a discussion on the research status of the entrepreneurial education field. It reviews the challenges and paradoxes of contemporary entrepreneurial education, as well as philosophical approaches and their growing acceptance. It also includes a review of the teaching methods in entrepreneurial education and underlines the importance of context for entrepreneurial learning. The third chapter demonstrates long-term trends in the field in terms of the content, methods and approaches used in entrepreneurial education research. It includes cross-sectional data; therefore, it enables the reader to gain an overview of the field and critically evaluate its progress. The fourth chapter includes a discussion of the achievements and failures of the field as well as on the future of entrepreneurial education as a research domain. The book ends with conclusions.

The contribution of this book is a research-based view of the development of the discipline and its actual performance in terms of scientific output. A thorough analysis of the state of the art of entrepreneurial education results in rethinking the progress of entrepreneurial education, as well as determining its future. Consequently, the book serves as a solid reference point for all interested in conducting research on entrepreneurial education or engaged in teaching entrepreneurship.

With the development of the field, the expectations towards it become higher. The critical tone of this introduction and the call for more rigour in research are signs of concern for its future and a belief that entrepreneurial education has the potential to become a distinct scholarly field. Being in vogue in academia stimulates more attention and popularity as well as greater responsibility for the reliability of research and the power of findings. Only when we ask about scholarly progress, can we develop the field further towards achieving the desired quality of scientific knowledge built on a sound intellectual basis. We intend to present recommendations for future research and clarify them to support scholars who continue to study the phenomenon of entrepreneurial education.

In this book, we decided to employ the term entrepreneurial education (Erkkilä, 2000) and therefore we refer to both a narrower and broader understanding of pedagogies supporting entrepreneurship. We are aware of the different perspectives on entrepreneurial education, which usually centre around the following two terms: *entrepreneurship education* and *enterprising education*. We discuss these differences and their consequences for the development of the field in the second chapter. However, the principal aim of this book is to cover the field as the integrated whole therefore we do not prioritize any of them, nor do we limit our research to only one of these perspectives.

The book is intended for a wide audience; however, it is primarily written for scholars and teachers/instructors in entrepreneurship and the entrepreneurial education field. The book is a research-based source of knowledge on the development of the field, as well as a practical guide to what needs to be considered when designing entrepreneurial education courses. The book is relevant to any type and level of course related to entrepreneurial education, both as an academic field and part of vocational training.

References

Blenker, P., Elmholdt, S. T., Frederiksen, S. H., Korsgaard, S., & Wagner, K. (2014). Methods in entrepreneurship education research: a review and integrative framework. *Education + Training, 56*(8/9), 697–715.

Erkkilä, K. (2000). *Entrepreneurial education: mapping the debates in the United States, the United Kingdom and Finland.* London: Garland, Taylor & Francis.

Fayolle, A. (2013). Personal views on the future of entrepreneurship education. *Entrepreneurship & Regional Development, 25*(7–8), 692–701.

Fayolle, A., Verzat, C., & Wapshott, R. (2016). In quest of legitimacy: the theoretical and methodological foundations of entrepreneurship education research. *International Small Business Journal, 34*(7), 895–904.

Fayolle, A., Landstrom, H., Gartner, W. B., & Berglund, K. (2016). The institutionalization of entrepreneurship: questioning the status quo and regaining hope for entrepreneurship research. *Entrepreneurship & Regional Development, 28*(7–8), 477–486.

Foliard, S., Pontois, S. L., Fayolle, A., & Diermann, I. (2018). The legitimacy of teachers in entrepreneurship education: what we can learn from a literature review. In *Creating entrepreneurial space: talking through multi-voices, reflections on emerging debates* (pp. 7–23). Emerald Publishing Limited: Bingley, UK.

Frank, H., & Landström, H. (2016). What makes entrepreneurship research interesting? Reflections on strategies to overcome the rigour–relevance gap. *Entrepreneurship & Regional Development, 28*(1–2), 51–75.

Hägg, G., & Gabrielsson, J. (2019). A systematic literature review of the evolution of pedagogy in entrepreneurial education research. *International Journal of Entrepreneurial Behavior & Research, 26*(5), 829–861.

Hägg, G., & Kurczewska, A. (2019). Who is the student entrepreneur? Understanding the emergent adult through the pedagogy and andragogy interplay. *Journal of Small Business Management, 57*(S1), 130–147.

Hägg, G., & Kurczewska, A. (2020). Towards a learning philosophy based on experience in entrepreneurship education. *Entrepreneurship Education & Pedagogy, 3*(2), 129–153.

Jones, C. (2006). Enterprise education: revisiting Whitehead to satisfy Gibbs. *Education + Training, 48*(5), 356–367.

Jones, C. (2019). A signature pedagogy for entrepreneurship education. *Journal of Small Business Enterprise Development, 26*(2), 243–254.

Katz, J. A. (2008). Fully mature but not fully legitimate: a different perspective on the state of entrepreneurship education. *Journal of Small Business Management, 46*(4), 550–566.

Kyrö, P. (2015). The conceptual contribution of education to research on entrepreneurship education. *Entrepreneurship & Regional Development, 27*(9–10), 599–618.

Landström, H. (2020). The evolution of entrepreneurship as a scholarly field. *Foundations and Trends in Entrepreneurship, 16*(2), 65–243.

Morris, M. H., & Liguori, E. (2016). *Annals of entrepreneurship education and pedagogy–2016*. Cheltenham, UK: Edward Elgar.

Nabi, G., Liñán, F., Fayolle, A., Krueger, N., & Walmsley, A. (2017). The impact of entrepreneurship education in higher education: a systematic review and research agenda. *Academy of Management Learning & Education, 16*(2), 277–299.

Neck, H. M., & Corbett, A. C. (2018). The scholarship of teaching and learning entrepreneurship. *Entrepreneurship Education & Pedagogy, 1*(1), 8–41.

Pittaway, L., & Cope, J. (2007). Entrepreneurship education a systematic review of the evidence. *International Small Business Journal, 25*(5), 479–510.

Rideout, E. C., & Gray, D. O. (2013). Does entrepreneurship education really work? A review and methodological critique of the empirical literature on the effects of university-based entrepreneurship education. *Journal of Small Business Management, 51*(3), 329–351.

1 The Brief History of Entrepreneurial Education

1.1 The Historical Context of the Rise of Entrepreneurial Education

Entrepreneurial education is a young field. One can even assume that it is one of the youngest among other sub-disciplines of education. However, it is difficult to precisely determine the beginning of entrepreneurial education as an academic field and as teaching practice. It is possible to find elements of both as far back as the middle of 20th century. Katz (2003) reports that one of the first courses in entrepreneurship was organized at Harvard University in the United States in 1947 by Myles Mace. Others, such as McMullan and Long (1987), state that some elements of entrepreneurial education can be found as far back as 1938 at Kobe University in Japan. However, more identifiable movements towards its institutionalization as an academic subject are visible from the late 1970s and early 1980s, the period associated with a general rise in interest in entrepreneurship and small business. These were the years when the oil crisis (1973) and the energy crisis (1979) led to the stagnation of economic growth and inflation, where world leaders were seeking some alternatives to save local economies and fight the growing crisis. The economic situation in the Western world was also weakened by the dynamic growth of Asian economies offering much cheaper goods and products, which were squeezing their Western counterparts out of domestic markets. A historical contextualization of the birth and rise of entrepreneurial education is important, as its profile and development have been shaped by context, both within academia and by external views on its importance for societal development. It is important to study the unique close link between the socio-economic reality and an academic agenda from both historical and research perspectives. Such exploration provides a better understanding of the

DOI: 10.4324/9781003194972-1

field of entrepreneurial education and its evolution, which is the primary aim of this book.

The series of crises in the 1970s proved that large state-owned companies could not remain as effective as expected and new solutions to boost the economy were urgently needed. The natural shift led to small business, which soon became the centre of the new political approach to the economy introduced mostly in the Western world, mainly by Thatcher in the UK and Reagan in the US. It has been recently popularized as the neoliberal approach. Privatization, marketization, financialization and deregulation began on a large scale. The post-war Keynesian view of the state and the economy was replaced by the simple and persuasive neoliberal vision of free markets and competition in the economy, by liberal democracy in politics and by a belief in the power of the enterprising self on a societal level. The idea was to transform skilled workers into self-organized entrepreneurs working for themselves by opening their own businesses. To enhance entrepreneurial activities, the tax regime was relaxed; income and corporate taxes were cut to induce more investment and encourage aspiring entrepreneurs to act. At the same time, through the move from a welfare state form of governing rooted in liberalism, towards neoliberalism, individuals were given more responsibility for their future (Amable, 2011), which was grounded in the ideal of the enterprising self-promoted by policy (Keat & Abercrombie, 2011; Rose, 1996). Individualism from a neoliberal perspective meant that everyone is accountable for their own well-being and success (Harvey, 2005), through the idea that each individual is expected to make an enterprise of her/his own life (Rose, 1996) and transform into an enterprising self (Ball & Olmedo, 2013). Collective well-being was understood as the sum of individual well-being calculated by means of individual cost-benefit analysis.

Despite the quite hefty critique received by neoliberalism in more recent times, the late 1970s and 1980s opened up the era of entrepreneurship that still prevails. The golden age for all types of entrepreneurial activity and venture creation had begun. In public discourse, enterprising and competitive individuals became responsible for their own success in life, promoted by a cultural shift in the core values of how members of society should act, based on notions of individualism, individual liberty, consumerism and economically calculated rationality. Together, these core values gave birth to the rise of the enterprising self. The success of this normative transformation of how members of society should be calibrated was due to the politically neutral tone of the enterprising self, as it did not refer to any particular political ideology, but appealed to the basic assumptions of the contemporary human being through its aspirations of autonomy, personal fulfilment and the individual's right to find meaning in her/his existence through individual acts and choices (Rose, 1996). The foundations of an enterprising culture and a culture of self-care were quickly built. Foucault's (2008, p. 226) words accurately express how the socio-economic landscape has changed:

> The stake in all neoliberal analyses is the replacement every time of homo oeconomicus as partner of exchange with a homo oeconomicus as entrepreneur of himself, being for himself his own capital, being for himself his own producer, being for himself the source of [his] earnings.

The neoliberal approach altered human relations and introduced the perspective that individuals achieve what they deserve, whereas their faults are results of their deficiencies such as not being sufficiently entrepreneurial and competitive. Life is like an enterprise to be run and a career path to be planned. Popular slogans of that time, such as "I wasn't lucky, I deserved it", "Don't follow the crowd, let the crowd follow you" or "People keep looking to government for the answer and government is the problem", well reflect the above-mentioned changes that opened the path for entrepreneurialism to prevail.

1.2 Changes in the Research Landscape and Education: The Entrepreneurial Education Boom

The power of entrepreneurship and small business was quickly recognized by scholarly circles. The newness of the field as well as the growing institutional support made entrepreneurial education attractive for many scholars. The positive atmosphere and pioneering type of work enabled the formation of new communities that engaged in studying this phenomenon. It was in the late 1970s and the 1980s that entrepreneurship as an academic field in its own right started to emerge (Landström, 2020). From a research perspective, in 1979 David Birch published his famous report "The Job Generation Process" that gave an impetus for a general interest in entrepreneurship as the new driver of economic growth. It was preceded by the Bolton Committee Report in 1971 that laid a foundation for a small business support strategy in the UK. From the 1990s onwards, the interest was further fuelled by various international institutions, including the OECD as well as the European Commission, which highlighted the link between entrepreneurship and a nation's prosperity. Interestingly, the new paradigm resulted in a rebirth of the Austrian school of economics and a renewed interest in Schumpeter's works. The American school of supply was developed in the 1970s, inspired by the views of Schumpeter, whose ideas were directly related to entrepreneurship and the development of the Small and Medium Sized Enterprise (SME) sector. Capitalism is not guided by the "invisible hand of the market", but by the actions of entrepreneurs who are willing to take risks and whose individual undertakings allow them to overcome growth barriers. From the research perspective, the 1970s also saw the publication of Israel Kirzner's *Competition and Entrepreneurship* (1973), one of the most influential books on entrepreneurship, which is rooted in the Austrian School of Economics and addresses the importance of entrepreneurial alertness when identifying and exploiting opportunities. However, the field of entrepreneurship continued to weaken its early strong ties to economics and gazed towards other social sciences, such as psychology, sociology, anthropology and finally management. The interdisciplinary character of entrepreneurship as a research field has provoked both external and internal criticism of its academic maturity and legitimacy, but the practical nature of the phenomenon has also brought hopes of discovering its essence and an emerging discussion on its teachability was born.

All these multi-level socio-economic turbulences led to constant changes in higher education and to the proliferation of the neoliberal view of it, which did not only mean the focus on popularizing entrepreneurial education, but also a perception of higher education as a business and quasi market practice where profit orientation started to become an indicator of academia's efficiency and success (Fernández-Herrería & Martínez-Rodríguez, 2016). As noted by Olssen and Peters (2005), the traditional culture of open intellectual debate gave way to an institutional focus on performativity and measured outputs, which consequently led to academia being seen through the lenses of strategic planning, performance indicators and academic audits. Moreover, education started to be regarded more as a personal investment that would lead to success in life, overtrumping the previous purpose of higher education as an intellectual endeavour enabling individuals to follow their own path in life. Another worry expressed was that neoliberal governing created an implicit normalization of how individuals should act and behave (Lemke, 2001). Standardization, unification and economization were not what academia was used to. Moreover, the triple helix model of innovation initiated by Etzkowitz (1993) and Etzkowitz and Leydesdorff (1995) only further popularized and institutionalized university-industry-government cooperation and introduced the idea of a third mission of the university, based on a commercialization of academic output and cooperation with the world outside academia. Entrepreneurship started to appear not only in the classroom in the form of courses or programmes, but also through an umbrella concept, the "entrepreneurial university", aimed at applying entrepreneurship in each aspect of higher education, where HEIs focused on opening up university to industry and business. HEIs as a whole were expected to become entrepreneurial and entrepreneurial education was seen as a perfect type of mass intervention to achieve that.

In the 1980s and 1990s entrepreneurship and small business started to flourish. The trend was reflected in a higher interest in teaching entrepreneurship on the part of academia. According to Vesper (1993), in 1968 there were only 4 schools offering this type of education, 16 in 1970 but 370 in 1993. Solomon, Weaver and Fernald (1994) report that the number of schools grew from 263 in 1979 to 1,400 in 1992. The studies by Solomon et al. and Vesper differ in terms of the type of courses/ programmes taken into consideration, but both show an unprecedented high growth of entrepreneurial education. As Landström (2020) explains, in the US the early growth of courses was also the result of the extensive resources invested in entrepreneurial education programmes.

Entrepreneurial education was initially positioned in the business area, which meant that mainly business school students or those studying management/business administration were exposed to it. At that stage, entrepreneurship was regarded as a higher education subject and was only offered to lower education levels as part of vocational training (Ball, 1989). The dominant motive for the wide implementation of entrepreneurial education was to enable and facilitate social and economic transformation. The responsibility for the transformation was left to scholars, who had to design courses and programmes without being able to support their teaching with sound research. The situation was unique for academics in the sense that the socio-economic objectives were clearer and prioritized at the expense of educative goals. To overcome this situation a series of research on entrepreneurial education was launched, including various special issues in, amongst others, *Simulation & Gaming* by Jerome Katz, as well as the continuous special issue in *Education + Training* by Harry Matlay that emerged in 2000 and is still a large part of research dissemination (Gabrielsson, Hägg, Landström, & Politis, 2020).

1.3 Towards Academic Legitimization of Entrepreneurial Education

The scholarly field of entrepreneurship started to develop at a faster rate than entrepreneurial education, as at the beginning it was seen more as an individual commitment and business orientation, and less as a societal and educational phenomenon (Kyrö, 2006). In addition, the conceptual debate on entrepreneurial education is in fact a debate on the interplay between education and entrepreneurship research (Béchard & Toulouse, 1991; Kyrö, 2006), therefore entrepreneurial education is dependent on the development of both. Klapper and Tegtmeier (2010) found that one of the earliest research studies on entrepreneurial education was conducted in the early 1980s and resulted in several publications at Baylor University. Another significant event for the legitimization of entrepreneurial education was a conference held at Harvard University in 1985 titled "Entrepreneurship: What It Is and How to Teach It".

The social and economic context of the 1970s and 1980s shaped the birth and direction of entrepreneurial education. The need for a vehicle of socio-economic transformation and extra resources designated for its continued development across HEIs enabled the field to start on the path towards academic legitimization. However, the intellectual progression of entrepreneurial education was weakened by the fact that scholars attracted by its newness and unexplored character had very diverse backgrounds and a general interest in and knowledge of entrepreneurship rather than general education (Hägg & Gabrielsson, 2019). The fields of entrepreneurship and entrepreneurial education developed in parallel, with entrepreneurship ahead but also struggling in terms of a conceptual and methodological debate (see Fayolle, 2013; Rideout & Gray, 2013). As Pittaway and Cope (2007) noted, the lack of agreement on the definition of entrepreneurship did not stop it being implemented in educational settings. There were far fewer transitions of scholars from the general education field, which resulted in the lower scholarship of entrepreneurial education in its initial phase. The first doctoral theses started to appear in the 1990s, but as many of them were written in various national languages, their contribution to the development of the field was limited (Kyrö, 2006).

When we examine the field of entrepreneurial education retrospectively, it is evident that at the beginning the scholarly debates centred around what to teach and then how to teach, and it was not until the 1990s that scholars started to investigate the learning process *per se*. We can call these decades the formation period of entrepreneurial education. More advanced concepts building on the distinctiveness of the field started to appear early in the 21st century. The entrepreneurial education research map is still fragmented, but looking back over the 40 years that have passed since it first entered higher education, we find that the progress is sufficiently vast to synthetize its output. However, from the early stage entrepreneurial education has been considered innovative and progressive when it comes to teaching (Hägg & Gabrielsson, 2019; Neck & Corbett, 2018). As Hägg and Gabrielsson (2019) observed in their synthesizing paper on the evolution of pedagogy in entrepreneurial education, it is possible to identify a movement from fragmented debates starting in the 1980s and continuing in the 1990s, towards more homogeneity in research journals and core references. This is visible progress when compared to the results of the study by Béchard and Grégoire (2005), in which they argue that in terms of educational theories, research on entrepreneurial education is rather incomplete and mainly focuses on the economic and business content of the teaching.

At present, the expectation is that entrepreneurial education will dissociate from its own roots linked to neoliberalism and become politically neutral, as this leads to a complete legitimization of the research field. As Morris (2014) pointed out, despite the unquestionable progress in entrepreneurship education as a field of study, there is still a growing gap between the demand for and growth of entrepreneurship education and what is known to work effectively in entrepreneurship education.

Academic legitimization of entrepreneurial education is closely linked to the development of the surrounding community. Worldwide, the entrepreneurial education community is growing and is one of the largest if one considers it a sub-field of entrepreneurship. The sign of its maturity is the academic initiatives entirely devoted to entrepreneurial education. In Europe, all major conferences such as RENT, ISBE and the EURAM Annual Conference have tracks dedicated to entrepreneurial education scholars, with the 3E conference organized by the European Council for Small Business and Entrepreneurship (ECSB) solely dedicated to entrepreneurial education as the flagship conference. In the US, the annual USASBE conference has been moulded to respond to the needs of entrepreneurial education scholars and educators. In addition, there are other initiatives such as the California Entrepreneurship Educators Conference that takes place annually. The communities organize space to publish their research findings. Journals entirely devoted to entrepreneurial education are becoming established with the newly launched *Journal of Entrepreneurship Education and Pedagogy*, but more mature outlets have also published research on the topic and organized recurring special issues such as *Education + Training, Journal of Small Business and Management and Industry and Higher Education*. It is also worth mentioning the books published in a series by Edward Elgar, such as the *Annals of Entrepreneurship Education and Pedagogy* and the *Handbook of Research in Entrepreneurship Education*. All these international initiatives are supported by many national and local academic events.

In addition to the growing community of entrepreneurial education scholars, another sign of the maturity of a field is its ability to look inward and critically investigate its progress and direction by questioning taken-for-granted norms and assumptions (Fayolle, 2013). The more visible critical studies on entrepreneurship in general started to appear early in the first decade of the 21st century. They question the normative idea that entrepreneurship only constitutes a good phenomenon and that a greater number of entrepreneurs in society is always positive (Weiskopf & Steyaert, 2009). Therefore, they hit a neoliberal cord that had largely been unquestioned in the understanding of entrepreneurship and where the darker side of entrepreneurship was mainly passed over in silence. Criticism has also been levelled at the field of entrepreneurial education. For example, Farny, Frederiksen, Hannibal and Jones (2016) call for a more critical pedagogy to outweigh the cult of entrepreneurship in entrepreneurship education. Berglund and Verduyn (2018) identified two points in the critical approach to entrepreneurial education. The first is related to the critique of perceiving entrepreneurship as not a human but a market activity without providing an alternative view with a wider definition of entrepreneurship. The second point relates to the criticisms of the enterising self as a solution to not only individual but also societal problems. The critical studies on entrepreneurial education have maintained their momentum.

The critical approach to entrepreneurship as a phenomenon relates not only to its role in the economy, but also to its ethical side. Neoliberalism developed an ideal environment for a new type of company and a new type of entrepreneur. The unprecedented rapid and global expansion of these companies, their multimillion revenues, risky decisions and young people behind the success all contribute to the rise of super entrepreneurs, enhanced by media attention and approbation. With a view to launching unicorns, super entrepreneurs concentrate on how to disrupt the market and create novel business models. Although they succeed in a short time and on a spectacular scale, these entrepreneurial stories are both alluring and scary (an example is the rise and fall of Elisabeth Holmes and her blood testing company Theranos). Moreover, an admiration for unicorns and super entrepreneurs carries a risk for more ordinary entrepreneurs, who are often greatly influenced by them and treat them as role models. Therefore, questionable behaviour may be mimicked and misinterpretations of how to act can result in less positive outcomes, one of which is unethical behaviours, as they do not have any other point of reference or guidelines when engaging in the opportunity process. This could lead the more ordinary entrepreneur towards a state of disappointment and frustration, where shortcuts and less responsible entrepreneurial behaviour can become the reality. They are at risk of blindly following super entrepreneurs in their ventures without reflecting on the ethicality of the business intent and the consequences of their entrepreneurial actions.

1.4 On the Crossroads – Entrepreneurial Education Today and Tomorrow

When we compare today to the late 1970s and the 1980s, it becomes clear that the political landscape has changed and although neoliberalism is still overwhelmingly present, neoliberal governing has mutated and transformed in many different ways (see Harvey, 2005). Criticism of it is also more common now (where J. E. Stiglitz, N. Chomsky, N. Klein, T. Piketty and S. Žižek are the most prominent examples, although not always directly expressing their criticism). Today, the capitalistic function is described as contributing to the rising economic inequalities, hence the opposite to what it was supposed to do. Furthermore, worldwide, the economic elite strengthen their position and power, whilst the poor have no choice but to follow a predetermined path, where boundary crossing becomes more and more impossible. The asymmetry of information and capital has proved difficult to overcome and the answer to the question of what ideology can replace neoliberalism is not clear either.

The growing tendencies towards authoritarianism (or authoritarian capitalism as a political economic model) and nationalist populism do not look promising in economic and social terms, but their focus may weaken the priority of entrepreneurship (or at least some of its characteristics) on the political agenda, as it moves away from a neoliberal and entrepreneurial one. The global financial crisis of 2007 and 2008 showed the deficiencies of neoliberalism as an economic model glorifying multinational companies, banks and investment funds; however, it has not changed the wealth distribution and did not stop marketization processes across economies. Instead, the economic crisis created a perfect birth ground for a controversial phenomenon termed the gig economy (a workforce environment where temporary jobs are commonplace and companies tend to hire independent contractors and freelancers instead of full-time employees). The birth of the gig economy not only altered the labour market, but also enhanced the exploitive power of entrepreneurship, where the "giggers" are treated as subcontractors and deprived of many rights. Despite calls to abandon neoliberal ideals, the current development of the gig economy underlines the continuous need to understand the role that entrepreneurs play and the continuing importance of comprehending how entrepreneurial education could help foster entrepreneurial citizens.

The current call for degrowth and a sustainable economy, together with the environmental crisis, are changing the view on the role of economics and entrepreneurship. Sustainable and green entrepreneurship is seen as a potential solution to protect the future, but requires a total reconceptualization of entrepreneurship. Degrowth philosophy demands changes in production and consumption, which implies the need for new business models in many companies all over the world and necessitates a collapse of today's entrepreneurial culture. The translation of degrowth theory into business practice is a difficult task involving all three dimensions of sustainable development (economic, environmental and social) and its execution includes many contradictions and struggles. Rindova, Barry and Ketchen (2009) see a further development of the field in the emerging change from a focus on wealth creation as a primary motive for venture start-up. The change of the economic paradigm seems to be a matter of time, but it also requires deep restructuring of entrepreneurship and as a consequence, entrepreneurial education.

1.5 The Influence of Historical Context on the Perception of Entrepreneurial Education

The historical context and its development have influenced how entrepreneurial education is perceived at the present time. In recent years, it has started to be seen as a mouthpiece to promote capitalistic values connected to neoliberalism (Erkkilä, 2000; Rose, 1996), for which it has been criticized by many intellectuals and scholars. However, at the same time entrepreneurial education has been put into the situation where it needs to respond to numerous social needs. For example, preparing students to contribute to economic growth by creating their own businesses and building students' entrepreneurial awareness and confidence, as well as their responsibility for the consequences of entrepreneurial actions. It has been seen as a transformational intervention, argued to be essential for preparing the future generation of citizens for the fourth industrial revolution and the new world of work. The requirements and expectations imposed by society or rather policy makers on entrepreneurial education were (and still are) enormous when compared to other fields, even those with longer academic traditions and more experience of teaching. For example, we seldom question or ask other management disciplines to cater for individual development beyond the discipline. Because being entrepreneurial has been argued to be a key competence for 21st-century society, entrepreneurial education is expected to bring about long-term changes in individuals. From the outset, entrepreneurial education was not only about providing knowledge (about entrepreneurship) but also developing entrepreneurial skills and attitudes leading to venture creation. It was aimed at enhancing entrepreneurial thinking. However, cognitive changes require more time and effort from both learners and educators.

When the bar is placed so high and the time is limited, institutional pressure may result in imprudent and shortcut solutions. Therefore, some of the first attempts at educating might have been burdened with a higher probability of mistakes, especially when the lack of an existing repository of knowledge and expertise in the field is taken into consideration. Furthermore, the fact that it is practice oriented and influenced by a largely practitioner-driven perspective has hindered the field in building its academic legitimacy (Fayolle, Verzat, & Wapshott, 2016).

In the eyes of policy makers, the results of entrepreneurial education are relatively easy to test, such as the number of new companies set up by students or alumni, or by measuring the growth of entrepreneurial intentions among students exposed to this type of education. For a scholar trained in education science, evaluating education through such measures is problematic both content-wise and method-wise, as well as often being contrary to what is usually demanded from students in the learning process, especially as a long-term outcome.

Entrepreneurship has been presented as a vehicle for overcoming social and economic inequalities and a pass to a better world, where the rules are clear and much depends on the individual's hard work and motivation. Everybody can become an entrepreneur and steer her/his own life as business opportunities are everywhere and it is sufficient to identify and exploit them. The belief that societal and economic progress is ensured by maximizing individual profits is supported by the growing number of super entrepreneurs who succeed in a short time and on a spectacular scale. Entrepreneurship became fashionable and the entrepreneurial culture dominated not only university campuses but also the lifestyle of students. Moreover, courses in entrepreneurship were perceived as attractive as they involved some action, were less standardized than other more traditional courses and the pedagogy applied was more innovative (Sexton & Bowman-Upton, 1987). The activities within courses often took place outside the classroom, demanded teamwork and had a problem-based orientation demanding creativity and innovation. Entrepreneurship courses also fulfilled the need for more practice-based learning and introduced a new type of collaborative work, where individualized learning is enhanced by social learning, enabling different learning strategies to be adopted. Although the proportion between individuation and socialization in learning is debatable and the processes are very different in terms of courses and outcomes (Rorty, 1999), entrepreneurial education turned towards the latter. The positive perception of entrepreneurial education has been influenced by its strong emphasis on employability and close connection with future working life.

The problem that emerged over time is that despite in-depth studies on entrepreneurship and its different facets, only one version has dominated the public discourse, namely the one representing an individualistic or even egocentric type of entrepreneurial behaviour. The public gained an image of the entrepreneur who only concentrates on her/his own success. Other forms of entrepreneurship, such as social and sustainable, have only recently received increased attention and interest from policy makers. Previously, society-focused actions of entrepreneurs were described through the concept of Corporate Social Responsibility (CSR). Erkkilä (2000) claims that a limited understanding of entrepreneurship is common, therefore more efforts must be made to uncover its characteristics. Our understanding of entrepreneurship has also been greatly influenced by the American entrepreneurial culture, which in present times does not provide a good roadmap for the versatility of the phenomenon of entrepreneurial education that can be found across the globe.

1.6 Summary – Where Are We Today and How Has History Played a Part?

In the present chapter we have addressed our historical understanding surrounding the development of entrepreneurial education and the different factors that enabled entrepreneurial education to experience such exponential growth on a global scale. As explained by Landström (2020), history can be told in many ways and this is our interpretation of how different streams of literature have impacted the current hype and inclusion of entrepreneurialism and entrepreneurial education in modern society. Entrepreneurship gained traction from political governing due to the move from an embedded liberal policy towards a neoliberal policy where the entrepreneur and small business owner were positioned as a key to generate economic development in society. This change also made the responsibility for educating potential entrepreneurs and small business owners a central priority. Furthermore, in the early stage the field was largely developed by individual scholars as the area of study was not accepted as a legitimate academic subject and even today it has not yet gained full legitimacy (see Fayolle et al., 2016). The critical studies were largely lacking in the development of the field, but their presence has now increased due to the call for legitimacy and inward inspection of its own practice.

Owing to ethically questionable behaviour and the present doubts about neoliberal market capitalism where the entrepreneur has been praised, we might see a change in how the entrepreneur is viewed in society. There might soon be a new type of crossroads where it is no longer a question of the need for entrepreneurial education, but rather for what purpose entrepreneurial education should be pursued. The previous economic function where the entrepreneur and small business owner was the overriding goal is slowly altering towards a goal of self-development, where entrepreneurial competencies and becoming an agent of change are gaining ground. But how has this radical change come about? To address this there is a need to discuss the different views that currently exist on how to teach and learn, as well as the overriding objectives that have formed and matured in entrepreneurial education, which will be presented in the following chapter.

References

Amable, B. (2011). Morals and politics in the ideology of neo-liberalism. *Socio-Economic Review, 9*(1), 3–30.

Ball, C. (1989). *Towards an 'enterprising' culture: a challenge for education and training.* (4). Paris, France: OECD/CERI.

Ball, S. J., & Olmedo, A. (2013). Care of the self, resistance and subjectivity under neoliberal governmentalities. *Critical Studies in Education, 54*(1), 85–96.

Béchard, J.-P., & Grégoire, D. (2005). Entrepreneurship education research revisited: the case of higher education. *Academy of Management Learning & Education, 4*(1), 22–43.

Béchard, J.-P., & Toulouse, J.-M. (1991). Entrepreneurship and education: viewpoint from education. *Journal of Small Business & Entrepreneurship, 9*(1), 3–13.

Berglund, K., & Verduyn, K. (2018). *Revitalizing entrepreneurship education: adopting a critical approach in the classroom.* London: Routledge.

Birch, D. L. (1979). *The job generation process.* Cambridge, MA: M.I.T. Program on Neighborhood and Regional Change.

Bolton Committee Report (The) (1971). Small firms, report of the committee of inquiry on small firms, HMSO, CMND. 4811, London.

Erkkilä, K. (2000). *Entrepreneurial education: mapping the debates in the United States, the United Kingdom and Finland.* London: Garland, Taylor & Francis.

Etzkowitz, H. (1993). Technology transfer: The second academic revolution. Technology Access Report 6, 7–9.

Etzkowitz, H., & Leydesdorff, L. (1995). The triple helix – university-industry-government relations: a laboratory for knowledge-based economic development. *EASST Review 14*, 14–19.

Farny, S., Frederiksen, S. H., Hannibal, M., & Jones, S. (2016). A culture of entrepreneurship education. *Entrepreneurship & Regional Development, 28*(7–8), 514–535.

Fayolle, A. (2013). Personal views on the future of entrepreneurship education. *Entrepreneurship & Regional Development, 25*(7–8), 692–701.

Fayolle, A., Verzat, C., & Wapshott, R. (2016). In quest of legitimacy: the theoretical and methodological foundations of entrepreneurship education research. *International Small Business Journal, 34*(7), 895–904.

Fernández-Herrería, A., & Martínez-Rodríguez, F. M. (2016). Deconstructing the neoliberal 'Entrepreneurial Self': a critical perspective derived from a global 'biophilic consciousness'. *Policy Futures in Education, 14*(3), 314–326.

Foucault, M. (2008). *The birth of biopolitics: lectures at the Collège de France, 1978–1979*. London: Palgrave Macmillan.

Gabrielsson, J., Hägg, G., Landström, H., & Politis, D. (2020). Connecting the past with the present: the development of research on pedagogy in entrepreneurial education. *Education + Training, 62*(9), 1061–1086.

Harvey, D. (2005). *A brief history of neoliberalism*. New York: Oxford University Press.

Hägg, G., & Gabrielsson, J. (2019). A systematic literature review of the evolution of pedagogy in entrepreneurial education research. *International Journal of Entrepreneurial Behavior & Research, 26*(5), 829–861.

Katz, J. A. (2003). The chronology and intellectual trajectory of American entrepreneurship education: 1876–1999. *Journal of Business Venturing, 18*(2), 283–300.

Keat, R., & Abercrombie, N. (2011). *Enterprise culture*. London: Routledge.

Klapper, R., & Tegtmeier, S. (2010). Innovating entrepreneurial pedagogy: examples from France and Germany. *Journal of Small Business and Enterprise Development, 17*(4), 552–568.

Kyrö, P. (2006). The continental and Anglo-American approaches to entrepreneurship education – differences and bridges. In A. Fayolle & H. Klandt (Eds.), *International entrepreneurship education, issues and newness* (pp. 93–111). Cheltenham, UK; Northampton, MA: Edward Elgar Publishing.

Landström, H. (2020). The evolution of entrepreneurship as a scholarly field. *Foundations and Trends in Entrepreneurship, 16*(2), 65–243.

Lemke, T. (2001). 'The birth of bio-politics': Michel Foucault's lecture at the Collège de France on neo-liberal governmentality. *Economy and Society, 30*(2), 190–207.

McMullan, W., & Long, W. A. (1987). Entrepreneurship education in the nineties. *Journal of Business Venturing, 2*(3), 261–275.

Morris, M. H. (2014). *Preface: establishing moorings and foundations in entrepreneurial education, annals of entrepreneurship education and pedagogy*. Cheltenham, UK and Northampton, MA: Edward Elgar.

Neck, H. M., & Corbett, A. C. (2018). The scholarship of teaching and learning entrepreneurship. *Entrepreneurship Education & Pedagogy, 1*(1), 8–41.

Olssen, M., & Peters, M. A. (2005). Neoliberalism, higher education and the knowledge economy: from the free market to knowledge capitalism. *Journal of Education Policy, 20*(3), 313–345.

Pittaway, L., & Cope, J. (2007). Entrepreneurship education a systematic review of the evidence. *International Small Business Journal, 25*(5), 479–510.

Rideout, E. C., & Gray, D. O. (2013). Does entrepreneurship education really work? A review and methodological critique of the empirical literature on the effects of university-based entrepreneurship education. *Journal of Small Business Management, 51*(3), 329–351.

Rindova, V., Barry, D., & Ketchen, D. J. (2009). Entrepreneuring as emancipation. *Academy of Management Review, 34*(3), 477–491.

Rorty, R. (1999). *Philosophy and social hope.* London, UK: Penguin.

Rose, N. (1996). *Inventing our selves: psychology, power, and personhood.* Cambridge: Cambridge University Press.

Sexton, D. L., & Bowman-Upton, N. (1987). Evaluation of an innovative approach to teaching entrepreneurship. *Journal of Small Business Management, 25*(1), 35–43.

Solomon, G. T., Weaver, K. M., & Fernald, L. W. (1994). A historical examination of small business management and entrepreneurship pedagogy. *Simulation & Gaming, 25*(3), 338–352.

Vesper, K.H. (1993). *Entrepreneurship education.* Entrepreneurial Studies Center, UCLA, Los Angeles, CA.

Weiskopf, R., & Steyaert, C. (2009). Metamorphoses in entrepreneurship studies: towards an affirmative politics of entrepreneuring. In D. Hjorth & C. Steyaert (Eds.), *The politics and aesthetics of entrepreneurship* (pp. 183–201). Cheltenham, UK: Edward Elgar.

2 The Current Standing of Entrepreneurial Education

2.1 Different Views on Entrepreneurial Education

2.1.1 Entrepreneurship Education plus Enterprise Education = Entrepreneurial Education

To look broadly at the field, there are two approaches that define entrepreneurial education, which do not exist in isolation but are instead interrelated and have been developing in parallel as well as in tandem. These two approaches within entrepreneurial education derived from the way its goal and scope are defined and differ in the sense that one is a broad process aimed at developing enterprising individuals, while the second is a narrow start-up process. The first approach concerns forming enterprising individuals by developing their diverse qualities (such as knowledge and skills) as well as enhancing the flexibility, creativity and adaptability of organizations, communities, societies and cultures (Ball, 1989). The second approach, the narrower one, sees entrepreneurial education through the start-up process and the individual's journey creating and managing new ventures, as well as regarding it as curriculum development (Ball, 1989; Hägg, 2017). The first approach relates to the enterprising education school, whereas the second concerns the entrepreneurship education school. This division influences both the content of the courses and the research agenda. However, in our view, it does not influence the general progression of the field, as the research findings from both schools are not contradictory and do not cannibalize each other. Instead, they have contributed to the development of the field over time and despite their differences, their internal struggle has enriched the research discussion and provided seeds for the development of the field as a whole (see e.g., Hägg & Gabrielsson, 2019).

As briefly explained in the Introduction, we decided to follow the recommendation of Erkkilä (2000) and use the term "entrepreneurial

DOI: 10.4324/9781003194972-2

education", despite the fact that the terms "entrepreneurship education" and "enterprising education" seem to dominate in the literature. Even in the Google Scholar browser, entrepreneurship education receives 133,000 hits, enterprise education 30,300 and entrepreneurial education only 27,800 (as of February 2021). In general, enterprise education is more commonly used by British scholars, whereas their continental European and US counterparts tend to prefer entrepreneurship education. However, our intention is not to highlight any division of the field, but rather to show it as an integrated whole, and therefore we do not explore this division in depth and compare both perspectives.

2.1.2 Diverse Roles of Entrepreneurial Education – A Policy Tool or Lifelong Learning Agenda?

Since the emergence of the enterprise culture (Keat & Abercrombie, 1991) entrepreneurial education has attained a prominent position in society as an educational tool to spur economic growth and as an educational process to develop entrepreneurial individuals who are able to cope with the increased uncertainties that prevail in the globalized society we inhabit. Over time various views on what entrepreneurial education might mean have been formed, where the two main distinctions could be recognized in the critical school of thought that considers entrepreneurship as a neoliberal policy tool to govern members of society (Amable, 2011; Berglund & Verduyn, 2018; Foucault, 2008; Frederiksen & Berglund, 2020; Hägg & Schölin, 2018). However, from a more educational perspective, the pedagogical development of entrepreneurial education and its ability to challenge the prevailing norms on how to teach and educate in higher education has a stronger position as the view to which the majority of scholars adhere (Neck & Corbett, 2018), where the goal of developing strong and self-regulated learners who can face uncertainty and find solutions to societal problems is high on the agenda (Gibb, 2002; Hägg & Kurczewska, 2020b; Jones, 2019; Neck & Corbett, 2018). For a long time this view has challenged the prevailing view on how to educate in higher education, where experimentation and adoption of experience-based pedagogy have gained a primary position (Fayolle, 2013; Gundry & Kickul, 1996; Hägg & Gabrielsson, 2019; Jones, 2009; Sexton & Bowman-Upton, 1987). Over time different objectives have materialized, which mainly revolve around either how to identify and exploit entrepreneurial opportunities by means of starting a venture (Neck, Greene, & Brush, 2014) as well as within existing companies as intrapreneurs (Kuratko & Morris, 2018), or how to develop responsible entrepreneurial citizens who are able to take charge of their own lives as agents of change in society (Ball, 1989; Jones & Iredale, 2010; Jones, Matlay, Penaluna, & Penaluna, 2014). Although differences exist, there are underlying pedagogical practices and learning theories that unite these diverse views and learning objectives, which will be further addressed in the following section.

2.1.3 Entrepreneurial Education as a Process and Method

The development of entrepreneurship as a research field provided an understanding of entrepreneurship as a learning process, which in turn called for a theory of learning (Minniti & Bygrave, 2001). Learning exists within entrepreneurship (Cope, 2005; Corbett, 2005; Deakins & Freel, 1998; Politis, 2005b) and being a process of change in human behaviour and way of perceiving reality provides deeper understanding of how some individuals turn ideas into business ventures. The assumption is that within the entrepreneurial process entrepreneurs learn how to act and think in an entrepreneurial way. Learning is a process of mirroring how entrepreneurs learn. It may take place on both the individual and collective level (as organizational learning or team learning) and is a result of gaining experience. Therefore, looking at entrepreneurship as a learning process enables deconstruction of the entrepreneurial process. In the context of entrepreneurship education, the learning process has been understood as a mix of different elements leading to entrepreneurial competence (Gibb, 1993; Hägg, 2017). As a consequence, entrepreneurial learning is illustrated in two different modes: as an entrepreneurial process and as a way to gain entrepreneurial knowledge.

Another quite alternative view that has emerged in research on entrepreneurial education is to treat learning as a method. Neck and Greene (2011) claim that the method of teaching (understood both as a way of thinking and acting) *per se* might be more important than its content, particularly in an unpredictable world full of constant change. The authors compare teaching entrepreneurship as a method and as a process, which they describe as comprising known inputs and predictable outputs. They state that entrepreneurship education is a set of practices that goes beyond understanding, knowing and talking. It is a method involving systematic thinking and acting. Recommended techniques include start-up practices, serious games and simulations, design-based learning and reflective practice. The method approach bears similarities to the idea of effectuation (Sarasvathy & Venkataraman, 2011).

The method perspective has gained a foothold, as the functionalist paradigm in research has been strong for understanding entrepreneurship during the last two-three decades, but it is not necessarily fully on par with the educational perspective. However, regardless of whether one views entrepreneurial education as a process or a method there are underlying learning theories that unite these two views, which will be addressed in the following section.

2.2 The Research Status of Entrepreneurial Education

2.2.1 The Review of Learning Theories in Entrepreneurship Education

The Pragmatic Orientation in Entrepreneurial Education

With its roots in American culture, on an intellectual level entrepreneurial education was largely influenced by the American pragmatism movement, in particular from the works of John Dewey, who highlighted the importance of experience in learning processes. The fundamental characteristic of pragmatism is a practice orientation and striving for truth by a method of scientific inquiry, applying those concepts and hypotheses that become clearer tracing their practical consequences (Dewey, 1946). The fit between entrepreneurial education and the pragmatic approach resulted in the elevation of experience as a source of knowledge on entrepreneurship and in searching for new learning tools that could support a future-orientated education. For pragmatists, knowledge is in the present and lasts no longer than the point at which new evidence emerges that demonstrates its fallacy or incompleteness (Hägg & Kurczewska, 2020b). The same mechanism is present for entrepreneurship, as the experiences of an entrepreneur will not be relevant forever. Therefore, it is necessary to constantly collect meaningful experiences and learn how to generate knowledge from them.

Entrepreneurial Education as Progressive Education

Pragmatism was part of a progressive educational movement. Initially, the term "progressive" was used to contrast it to the education in the 20th century, which was termed traditional. In order to juxtapose progressive and traditional education, Dewey (1946, p. 83–84) wrote:

> Traditional education tended to ignore the importance of personal impulse and desire as moving springs. But this is no reason why progressive education should identify impulse and desire with purpose and thereby pass lightly over the need for careful observation, for wide range of information, and for judgment if students are to share in the formation of the purposes which activate them. In an educational scheme, the occurrence of a desire and impulse is not the final end. It is an occassion and a demand for the formation

Table 2.1 Traditional and progressive education

Traditional education	Progressive education
Focus on external discipline, education as imposed from above	Focus on free activity and individuality
Textbooks and teachers as main source of learning	Experience as a learning platform
Preparing for the future by following the achievements and heritage of past generations	Making the most of the opportunities in life
Static aims	Acquaintance with a changing world

Source: Inspired by Dewey (1946).

of a plan and method of activity. Such a plan, to repeat, can be formed only by study of conditions and by securing all relevant information.

The significant difference between the two lies in their time orientation. Progressive education is more grounded in the present and therefore seeks to solve more actual societal problems. Traditional education highlights the accomplishments of the past and the heritage of previous generations. Progressive education is built on the assumption that the world is constantly changing, thus education needs to be responsive and adjust to these changes. Only then can learners profit from opportunities that arise in their lives. The concept of progressive education is closely linked to ideas such as freedom, human development, active participation and democratic society. Progressive educators accentuate the significance of the individuality and autonomy of an individual. They claim learning is a continuous and never-ending process, flowing from one experience to another. This process is very individual and learner-oriented, but also related to a certain group of people, thus cooperative and collaborative.

Some other contrasting characteristics of progressive and traditional education are presented in Table 2.1.

The division between traditional and progressive education can also be observed to some extent in the paradigm difference between behaviourism and constructivism, which will be addressed next.

Constructivism as the Dominant Model of Education

In general, education comprises two competing models (or even paradigms) of learning, resulting in two theories of knowledge – behaviourism and constructivism. In the behaviouristic model, the assumption is that behaviour is predictable and controllable and therefore the research focuses on objective and measurable behaviours and how learning is influenced by changes in the environment. The idea is that through adequate learning interventions, all learners, being passive recipients, are able to possess the same rigid knowledge of the world (Löbler, 2006). In contrast, constructivism, which emerged as an outcome of cognitive development studies in psychology, is more interested in deeper understanding than acquiring information and memorizing facts. Learning is subjective in nature and aligned to the development of learners' awareness and consciousness, which enables them to adopt a critical stance, question what is known and to reflect on the unknown. It takes place through interaction with others and gives meaning to the world and one's own life. Learners mostly gain knowledge through experiences by using mental schemas, where accumulating experiences broadens and changes their knowledge structures. However, constructivism is a broad term, which over time developed two streams of the theory. The first is related to individual cognition and the individual act of trying to make sense of the world, whereas the second refers to the socialized learning and socially situated context of cognition (Mueller & Anderson, 2014). Both relate well to the characteristics of entrepreneurial education and highlight the idea that "learning is constructed by the individual to transform acquired cognition into knowledge" (Mueller & Anderson, 2014).

Why do constructivism and social constructivism fit entrepreneurial education, thus making them popular among entrepreneurial education scholars? The main reason is the novel approach to learning, compared to the traditional, behaviouristic one that dominates in many other fields. The constructivist model serves as a foundation for entrepreneurial education as it focuses on action learning, experiential learning and problem-based learning, hence forms of learning corresponding with the progressive and pragmatic nature of entrepreneurial learning. It also posits the student and the learning process at the centre of attention (Krueger, 2007). As Löbler (2006) argues, within the constructivist model learners not only create but also govern their own learning process, which is open for any type of content, style, goal and experience. This type of education makes them responsible for learning as well as enables them to answer all questions of concern. In practice, the constructivist approach involves learning as a self-governed, on-going process, which means that teaching supports learning and the learner is an active producer, while the teacher is more like an assistant in learners' learning processes (Löbler, 2006). Within constructivism, entrepreneurial learning is based on constructing cognitive schemas based on experiences and changing knowledge structures while searching for meaning. Therefore, experiences enable changes in knowledge structures. In research terms, when emphasis is placed on learners' knowledge construction, the studies on learning are aimed at providing explanations of how individuals can learn from experience (Mueller & Anderson, 2014).

Constructivism is often associated with transformative learning (Mezirow, 1991) where, in the context of entrepreneurial education, the deep transformative episodes within the very personalized learning activities guide learners to entrepreneurial action and reflection. Learners are encouraged to engage in critical reflection, which if performed thoroughly gives meaning to learners and a deepened understanding of their lives. This also reflects the characteristics of entrepreneurial education, where the goal is to transform the learner into an entrepreneurial individual who is able to take entrepreneurial decisions and actions and, in the long term, leading to sustained entrepreneurial behaviour or the development of an entrepreneurial mindset, two aspects that often go hand in hand.

Importantly, an interest in constructivism and the transformative potential of education enabled entrepreneurial education research to create an action orientation in learning and teaching, as well as paved way for various experience-based pedagogical approaches, including action learning, experiential learning and problem-based learning, which will be discussed in the section that follows. A summary of the three learning theories can be seen in Table 2.2.

Table 2.2 Action-, experiential- and problem-based learning

Aspect/theory	Action learning	Experiential learning	Problem-based learning
Main definition	No main definition, instead a learning equation (Revans, 2011): $L = P + Q$ L = learning P = programmed knowledge Q = questioning insight	"The process whereby knowledge is created through the transformation of experience. Knowledge results from the combination of grasping and transforming experience" (Kolb, 1984, p. 41)	"Learning results from the process of working toward the understanding or resolution of a problem. Problems refers to an unsettled or puzzling issue that needs to be resolved, encountered in learning, as stimulus for problem-solving" (Barrows & Tramblyn, 1980, p. 18)
Key contributors	Pedler et al. (2005) Revans (2011)	Kolb (1984) Kolb & Kolb (2009)	Barrows & Tramblyn (1980) Schmidt (1993)
Core assumptions	• Learner centred • Experience • Team learning	• Learner centred • Experience • Individual learning	• Learner centred • Experience • Group learning

Aspect/theory	Action learning	Experiential learning	Problem-based learning
Similarities	• Reflection: key part of the learning process • Experience is important for the learner	• Reflection: key part of the learning process • Experience is important for the learner	• Reflection: key part of the learning process • Experience is important for the learner
Differences	• Organizational learning • Team learning • Individual problems, but team solution	• Individual learning • Learning cycle • Learning styles	• Education perspective • Small groups and collaborative learning • Predefined problems
Central concepts	• Team learning • Action • Critical questioning • Reflection	• Individual learning • Experiential learning cycle • Act, observe, abstract, experiment	• Defined problems • Fictional and live cases • Small group tutorials • Reasoning and reflection
Origins and roots	Developed by Reg Revans in Britain during the 1970s as an educational intervention in organization and management. Rooted in the thoughts of Lewin and Dewey (Marsick & O'Neil, 1999).	Developed by Kolb (1984), and rooted in the theories of Dewey, Lewin, Piaget and Freire. Broad focus on all types of education. Kolb developed a learning style inventory in connection with his experiential learning theory.	Developed at the McMaster University medical school in the 1960s (Neufeld & Barrows, 1974). It evolved through an innovative health science curricula (Savery, 2006), and is based on the Harvard case method. Its roots are found in Dewey's progressive educational movement.
Application in entrepreneurship education	• Main influence from British scholars • Enterprise learning	• Influential through entrepreneurial learning • Learning-by-doing	• Tested and applied as a teaching method for students interested in becoming entrepreneurs
Key research in entrepreneurship	Jones-Evans, Williams & Deacon (2000) Pittaway & Cope (2007) Rae (2009)	Cope & Watts (2000) Politis (2005a, 2005b) Corbett (2005, 2007) Dhliwayo (2008)	Hansemark (1998) Wee (2004) San Tan & Ng (2006) Krueger (2007)

Source: Hägg (2017, p. 36).

Action Learning

The pragmatic and progressive trend in education, strengthened by the constructivist model of education, turned entrepreneurial education into action and action-based pedagogy (Fiet, 2001a, 2001b;

Rasmussen & Sørheim, 2006). According to Revans, who pioneered the idea of action learning, its aim is not only learning *per se* but also change that will facilitate better future actions and outcomes. Therefore, action learning is applied in order to achieve constant progress (Revans, 1982). The idea of dialogical and purposeful learning is close to the expectations of entrepreneurial education scholars.

In simple words, actions mean what humans do. As already noted by the ancient Greeks, humans perform diverse actions, both unconscious and purposeful, as well as involuntary and autonomous ones (Thomson, Tredennick, & Barnes, 2004). In the context of entrepreneurship and entrepreneurial ventures, action is perceived as a result of intentional and planned behaviour, hence scholarly curiosity centres around purposeful actions, not "happenings" or mechanical reactions to some stimulus (Hägg & Kurczewska, 2016). This also explains and rationalizes the research devoted to exploring entrepreneurial intentions (as a proxy of entrepreneurs' intentional actions) and their antecedents in an entrepreneurial education context (for a meta-analysis of the relationship between entrepreneurship education and entrepreneurial intentions, see Bae, Qian, Miao and Fiet [2014]).

However, as Hägg and Kurczewska (2016) noted, the action orientation resulted in a ripple effect among entrepreneurship educators, who included acting as an important part when designing courses and curriculums without sufficient consideration of what action means in the entrepreneurial context and how it interacts with other elements within the learning process. The concern is that the term "action" has been interpreted and applied to learning process in too simplistic a way. Narrowing the learning process to "doing" may result in moving away from the essence of learning, which is knowledge creation.

Experiential Learning

The development of action orientation in the initial phase of entrepreneurial education also saw the inclusion of experiential learning, with a main emphasis on the theories of David A. Kolb and his seminal book published in 1984. The idea of experiential learning theory suited the insights that were developed during the 1980s on how entrepreneurs behave and act. Hence, the link between entrepreneurial learning and experiential learning theory was very much in symbiosis during the growth of entrepreneurship as a research field in the 1990s and early 2000s, where lived experience and the role of experimenting attained a primary position when addressing the learning behaviour of practicing entrepreneurs (Corbett, 2005; Deakins & Freel, 1998; Minniti

& Bygrave, 2001; Politis, 2005b). During the growth stage of entrepreneurial education in the 1990s the influence of experiential learning also gained traction in the educational context, where simulations and other practical learning activities sought to mirror the actual practice of entrepreneurs (Gundry & Kickul, 1996; Katz, Gundry, Low, & Starr, 1994). The idea of Kolb's (1984) learning cycle gained a foothold and became the main contributor to the current taken-for-granted assumption on experience as a driver of entrepreneurial learning in entrepreneurial education.

Problem-based Learning

Another perspective on entrepreneurial education refers to perceiving entrepreneurial learning as "a problem solving process centred on the acquisition, storage and use of entrepreneurial knowledge in long term memory" (Rae & Carswell, 2001, p. 221), thus fostering entrepreneurial thinking. Problem-based learning is a part of action-oriented pedagogy, which positions the learners and learning process at the centre of attention. As a learning theory, it demands critical but constructive thinking from learners, leading to knowledge construction. It is based on active learning situated in a specific context (Barrows, 1996). The fundamental idea of problem-based learning is to put students, often working in teams, into a situation where they face open-ended problems and support their efforts to find solutions. Instructors usually chose problems related to actual real world situations (often in the form of cases) that correspond to the theme addressed within the curriculum, although at the same time not self-evident and even provoking cognitive conflicts in learners. Problem-based learning also prepares learners for future entrepreneurial life as it creates some foundations of entrepreneurial knowledge in a way that is similar to how entrepreneurs acquire knowledge (Hägg, 2017). Krueger (2007) argues that the high value of problem-based learning in the context of entrepreneurial education is that it expects learners to move from answer-finding to question-creating, which translates into taking cognitive ownership of projects. He further argues that:

> Faced with very high uncertainty, extreme time pressures and competing demands on their time and effort, problem based learning mirrors what an entrepreneur faces on a daily basis. As students proceed, their reflections invariably lead them to that realization: the necessity for further improving their personal role identity as an entrepreneur.
>
> (Krueger, 2007, p.132)

Experience-based Learning

Contemporary, experience-based learning theories and pedagogy are considered the basic conceptual foundation for entrepreneurship education. Experiential education is a theoretical and philosophical framework (Itin, 1999; Roberts, 2012) that focuses on both curricula design and student learning (Hägg, 2017). It is an umbrella theory that starts from an understanding of the educational process as a whole, based on a similar argumentation to that of constructive alignment (Biggs & Tang, 2011), but with a different discussion on how the various learning activities create continuity between each other to generate what Dewey (1946) termed educative experiences. The idea behind experience-based learning and its links to entrepreneurial education (see Hägg, 2017) is a theoretical notion that emerged from Deweyan progressivism and contemporary discussions on experiential education (Roberts, 2012), but with additional elements introduced from cognitive load theory (Sweller, Ayres, & Kalyuga, 2011; Sweller, Kirschner, & Clark, 2007), which help us to understand the process and development from a learner's perspective and its interplay with the subject matter (Hägg & Kurczewska, 2019, 2020b).

The elementary assumption behind experiential learning in the context of entrepreneurial education is that entrepreneurs learn from past experiences. Therefore, entrepreneurial knowledge is generated and accumulated through experiences, where entrepreneurial learning is formed through an interplay between primary and secondary experiences (Hägg & Kurczewska, 2020b). This interplay builds on the central pillar constructed by Dewey (1946) when developing his thoughts on progressive education. In his reasoning he built on the dialectics between knowing and doing, arguing that one needs to know in order to do, and to do in order to know (McLellan & Dewey, 1889). It is the elements of physical experience and mental experience that together enable a continuous educative learning process. The idea of including experience in entrepreneurial education has a long tradition, which is mainly derived from Kolb (1984) and his experiential learning theory. The inclusion of experience took a similar approach to that of action, starting from the life world of practicing entrepreneurs and their behaviour. However, while experience-based learning with a foundation in experiential education takes experience as the primary vehicle for learning, it builds the process on a foundation in the educational literature and the difference between a learner and a practitioner (Sweller, 2015).

2.2.2 Entrepreneurial Education: Pedagogy and Andragogy as Two Sides of the One Coin

In the above discussion we have outlined the development of entrepreneurial education and the movement from a behaviouristic view on education to a more and more (co-)constructivist perspective on how learners learn. This was addressed by Krueger (2007) in the four-stage pedagogical evolution: (1) teacher-centred, (2) teaching-centred, (3) learner-centred and (4) learning-centred, where each stage moves the needle more and more from a behaviouristic towards a constructivist perspective on learning. In this development entrepreneurial education has included plenty of pedagogical and andragogical theories for how learning might take place. A main agenda has been the insights derived during the 1980s that entrepreneurs and small business owners learn through experience when practicing the profession (Ronstadt, 1985; Sexton & Bowman-Upton, 1987). These early insights opened up for pedagogical development and an upsurge of interest in testing different learning activities with a varied foundation in experience-based learning theories in the entrepreneurial classroom (Katz et al., 1994; Solomon, Weaver, & Fernald, 1994). This experimentation has continuously developed the research field of entrepreneurial education, which has been acknowledged as a progressive field when it comes to making the shift from teacher-led towards student-centred education (Robinson, Neergaard, Tanggaard, & Krueger, 2016). However, there has been a continuous call for merging the insights about practicing entrepreneurs with the knowledge already developed in the field of education (Béchard & Toulouse, 1991; Fayolle, 2013; Pittaway & Cope, 2007). In addition, there have been calls to strengthen the pedagogical side to create more understanding of what is learnt, how it is learnt, why it is learnt and for what reasons students learn.

In the strive for development and learning innovation there has been a continuous movement towards implementing and championing experience-based learning theories, where the ideas related to adult education have also received increased attention due to their close ties to learning from experience (Hägg & Kurczewska, 2020b; Pittaway, Missing, Hudson, & Maragh, 2009). The andragogical literature, where transformative learning by Jack Mezirow and also action learning with its foundation in business practice, has largely been promoted as an archetype for the context that entrepreneurial students should encounter when moving from a pedagogical towards an andragogical perspective on learning (Neck & Corbett, 2018). As a result, the scholarly discussion on the method in entrepreneurship education has centred around praising andragogy as the most adequate way to educate, where instructions relate more to the experiential process than to the content of the subject of entrepreneurship. In this vein, learners are treated as motivated, self-directed adults responsible for their learning and learning is considered a lifelong process of continuing inquiry.

However, the pedagogy, andragogy and to some extent the heutagogical discussion is not black and white but more about meeting students at their level of development (Hägg & Kurczewska, 2020a; Jones, Penaluna, & Penaluna, 2019). Hence, the ongoing debate in entrepreneurial education is not a winner take all game, where the loudest argument for a specific position and learning theory wins, but rather a discussion about a balanced act that can tailor educational learning processes based on meeting students at their level (Hägg & Kurczewska, 2019). Such an approach assumes that both pedagogy and andragogy are needed for understanding how the systematic process of education generates a fruitful learning process for students who undertake education in entrepreneurship. It is through the interplay of pedagogy and andragogy that we can understand how learning is developed in entrepreneurship education at university level, as it occurs when students are in transition from adolescence towards adulthood. In this respect, the hidden interplay between pedagogy and andragogy becomes a key as the focus in entrepreneurship education has gradually shifted from didactical content on what to teach towards the implementation of adult learning methods based on how practicing entrepreneurs learn, in addition to the recent inclusion of pedagogical insights on how to tailor the educational process. The challenge is the actual match between the maturity of learners and the methods used (and types of instruction), therefore the question is whether an andragogical perspective on learning is adequate for students who, in a majority of cases, are in a transitional stage between adolescence and adulthood.

2.3 The Role of Context in Entrepreneurial Education

The discussion on the role of context in entrepreneurial education refers to two aspects. The first is connected with the differing understanding of entrepreneurship in different cultures and environments, as well as its impact on the content of entrepreneurial education. Secondly, entrepreneurial education should be analysed in the context of the development of entrepreneurship research that addresses the contextual difference of sub-disciplines in entrepreneurship, such as corporate entrepreneurship, social-, eco-, migrant-, sport-, engineering- and arts-entrepreneurship.

As Erkkilä (2000) observed, there are many interpretations of entrepreneurial education, which differ within national and even local contexts. Entrepreneurship is culturally and experientially acquired (Hynes, 1996). The cultural context is argued to influence the development of entrepreneurial skills, but there are also variations between countries because of their different understanding of entrepreneurship (Leitch, Hazlett, & Pittaway, 2012; Welter, 2011). Likewise, Kurczewska, Kyrö and Abbas (2014) who conducted the study on the structural conditioning of entrepreneurship education and students' understanding of entrepreneurship in Finland and Egypt, argue that the level and character of entrepreneurship education is the result of the particular country's socio-economic situation and cultural background. The authors claim that entrepreneurial education is connected to the structure of society. However, at the same time, national characteristics make entrepreneurial education difficult to compare internationally.

The relation between entrepreneurship and education is changing in historical and geographical terms (Ball, 1989; Erkkilä, 2000; Gibb, 1993). As the birth and rise of entrepreneurial education was a result of the socio-economic changes of the late 1970s and the 1980s, the changes in entrepreneurial education are associated with fluctuations in the global, social, political and technological environment (Welsh, Tullar, & Nemati, 2016). The discussion on broad and narrow forms of entrepreneurial education addresses the two contextual differences in whether to educate towards enterprising individuals that transcend the educational space and where attention is on developing qualities to create enterprising competencies that can be applied in all walks of life (Jones & Iredale, 2010). However, on the other hand there is also the narrower context that starts from the subject domain of entrepreneurship research. Although the early discussions mainly centred around venture creation (e.g., Ronstadt, 1985), the contextual development has broadened in scope and the arrival of corporate entrepreneurship has gradually gained increased attention due to economic developments and the need for mid-sized and large corporations to stay agile and entrepreneurial (Kuratko & Morris, 2018).

Entrepreneurship as practice is always influenced by context. It is limited by the general economic and social circumstances, as well as by the situation and profile of the entrepreneur-to-be. Therefore, the task of the teacher is to teach students to recognize contexts with all their nuances and complexities in order to be able to respond to and even profit from them. To better understand the phenomenon of context in entrepreneurship, Thomassen, Middleton, Ramsgaard, Neergaard and Warren (2019) conducted a literature review on how context has been approached in research and on how context can be applied in entrepreneurial education. They recognize three levels of context: macro, meso and micro, with diverse elements on each of these levels. What is particularly interesting is the authors' conclusion that there is "no real *ceteris paribus* in entrepreneurship education", thus acknowledging that the importance of context means accepting that everything is not the same.

At the same time, considering context on a research level leads to the problem of generalization as context translates to some extent into the relativism of the investigated phenomenon. In turn, relativism makes it difficult to find a common framework. In this sense, we may conclude that contextualization might moderate the research because of context-specific nuances, but it is necessary in order to make educational practice relevant and up to date.

References

Amable, B. (2011). Morals and politics in the ideology of neo-liberalism. *Socio-Economic Review, 9*(1), 3–30.

Bae, T. J., Qian, S., Miao, C., & Fiet, J. O. (2014). The relationship between entrepreneurship education and entrepreneurial intentions: a meta-analytic review. *Entrepreneurship Theory & Practice, 38*(2), 217–254.

Ball, C. (1989). *Towards an 'enterprising' culture: a challenge for education and training*. (4). Paris, France: OECD/CERI.

Barrows, H. S. (1996). Problem-based learning in medicine and beyond: a brief overview. *New Directions for Teaching and Learning, 1996*(68), 3–12.

Barrows, H. S., & Tramblyn, R. M. (1980). *Problem-based learning: An approach to medical education*. New York: Springer Publishing.

Béchard, J.-P., & Toulouse, J.-M. (1991). Entrepreneurship and education: viewpoint from education. *Journal of Small Business & Entrepreneurship, 9*(1), 3–13.

Berglund, K., & Verduyn, K. (2018). *Revitalizing entrepreneurship education: adopting a critical approach in the classroom*. London: Routledge.

Biggs, J., & Tang, C. (2011). *Teaching for quality learning at university: what the student does* (4th ed.). New York: Open University Press.

Cope, J. (2005). Toward a dynamic learning perspective of entrepreneurship. *Entrepreneurship Theory & Practice, 29*(4), 373–397.

Cope, J., & Watts, G. (2000). Learning by doing–an exploration of experience, critical incidents and reflection in entrepreneurial learning. *International Journal of Entrepreneurial Behaviour & Research, 6*(3), 104–124.

Corbett, A. C. (2005). Experiential learning within the process of opportunity identification and exploitation. *Entrepreneurship Theory & Practice, 29*(4), 473–491.

Corbett, A. C. (2007). Learning asymmetries and the discovery of entrepreneurial opportunities. *Journal of Business Venturing, 22*(1), 97–118.

Deakins, D., & Freel, M. (1998). Entrepreneurial learning and the growth process in SMEs. *The Learning Organization, 5*(3), 144–155.

Dewey, J. (1946). *Experience and education.* New York: Macmillan.

Dhliwayo, S. (2008). Experiential learning in entrepreneurship education: A prospective model for South African tertiary institutions. *Education + Training, 50*(4), 329–340.

Erkkilä, K. (2000). *Entrepreneurial education: mapping the debates in the United States, the United Kingdom and Finland.* New York: Garland, Taylor & Francis Group.

Fayolle, A. (2013). Personal views on the future of entrepreneurship education. *Entrepreneurship & Regional Development, 25*(7–8), 692–701.

Fiet, J. O. (2001a). The pedagogical side of entrepreneurship theory. *Journal of Business Venturing, 16*(2), 101–117.

Fiet, J. O. (2001b). The theoretical side of teaching entrepreneurship. *Journal of Business Venturing, 16*(1), 1–24.

Foucault, M. (2008). *The birth of biopolitics: lectures at the Collège de France, 1978–1979.* London: Palgrave Macmillan.

Frederiksen, S. H., & Berglund, K. (2020). Identity work in entrepreneurship education: activating, scripting and resisting the entrepreneurial self. *International Small Business Journal, 38*(4), 271–292.

Gibb, A. A. (1993). Enterprise culture and education understanding enterprise education and its links with small business, entrepreneurship and wider educational goals. *International Small Business Journal, 11*(3), 11–34.

Gibb, A. A. (2002). Creating conducive environments for learning and entrepreneurship: living with, dealing with, creating and enjoying uncertainty and complexity. *Industry and Higher Education, 16*(3), 135–148.

Gundry, L. K., & Kickul, J. R. (1996). Flights of imagination: fostering creativity through experiential learning. *Simulation & Gaming, 27*(3), 334–349.

Hägg, G. (2017). Experiential entrepreneurship education: reflective thinking as a counterbalance to action for developing entrepreneurial knowledge. (PhD Compilation). Lund University, MediaTryck. (141)

Hägg, G., & Gabrielsson, J. (2019). A systematic literature review of the evolution of pedagogy in entrepreneurial education research. *International Journal of Entrepreneurial Behavior & Research, 26*(5), 829–861.

Hägg, G., & Kurczewska, A. (2016). Connecting the dots – a discussion on key concepts in contemporary entrepreneurship education. *Education + Training, 58*(7/8), 700–714.

Hägg, G., & Kurczewska, A. (2019). Who is the student entrepreneur? Understanding the emergent adult through the pedagogy and andragogy interplay. *Journal of Small Business Management, 57*(S1), 130–147.

Hägg, G., & Kurczewska, A. (2020a). Guiding the student entrepreneur – considering the emergent adult within the pedagogy–andragogy continuum in entrepreneurship education. *Education + Training, 62*(7/8), 759–777.

Hägg, G., & Kurczewska, A. (2020b). Towards a learning philosophy based on experience in entrepreneurship education. *Entrepreneurship Education & Pedagogy, 3*(2), 129–153.

Hägg, G., & Schölin, T. (2018). The policy influence on the development of entrepreneurship in higher education: a Swedish perspective. *Education + Training, 60*(7/8), 656–673.

Hansemark, O. C. (1998). The effects of an entrepreneurship programme on need for achievement and locus of control of reinforcement. *International Journal of Entrepreneurial Behaviour & Research, 4*(1), 28–50.

Hynes, B. (1996). Entrepreneurship education and training-introducing entrepreneurship into non-business disciplines. *Journal of European Industrial Training,* 20(8), 10–17.

Itin, C. M. (1999). Reasserting the philosophy of experiential education as a vehicle for change in the 21st century. *Journal of Experiential Education, 22*(2), 91–98.

Jones, B., & Iredale, N. (2010). Enterprise education as pedagogy. *Education + Training, 52*(1), 7–19.

Jones, C. (2009). Enterprise education: learning through personal experience. *Industry and Higher Education, 23*(3), 175–182.

Jones, C. (2019). A signature pedagogy for entrepreneurship education. *Journal of Small Business Enterprise Development, 26*(2), 243–254.

Jones-Evans, D., Williams, W., & Deacon, J. (2000). Developing entrepreneurial graduates: an action-learning approach. *Education + Training, 42*(4/5), 282–288.

Jones, C., Penaluna, K., & Penaluna, A. (2019). The promise of andragogy, heutagogy and academagogy to enterprise and entrepreneurship education pedagogy. *Education + Training, 61*(9), 1170–1186.

Jones, C., Matlay, H., Penaluna, K., & Penaluna, A. (2014). Claiming the future of enterprise education. *Education + Training, 56*(8/9), 764–775.

Katz, J. A., Gundry, L., Low, M., & Starr, J. (1994). Guest editorial: simulation and experiential learning in entrepreneurship education. *Simulation & Gaming, 25*(3), 335–337.

Keat, R., & Abercrombie, N. (1991). *Enterprise culture.* Abingdon, Oxon: Routledge.

Kolb, D. A. (1984). *Experiential learning: experience as the source of learning and development* (Vol. 1). Englewood Cliffs, NJ: Prentice-Hall.

Kolb, A. Y., & Kolb, D. A. (2009). The learning way meta-cognitive aspects of experiential learning. *Simulation & Gaming, 40*(3), 297–327.

Krueger, N. F. (2007). What lies beneath? The experiential essence of entrepreneurial thinking. *Entrepreneurship Theory & practice, 31*(1), 123–138.

Kuratko, D. F., & Morris, M. H. (2018). Corporate entrepreneurship: a critical challenge for educators and researchers. *Entrepreneurship Education & Pedagogy, 1*(1), 42–60.

Kurczewska, A., Kyrö, P., & Abbas, A. (2014). Transformative capacity of entrepreneurship education in two different cultural settings – morphogenetic analysis of Egypt and Finland. *Journal of Enterprising Culture, 22*(4), 401–435.

Leitch, C., Hazlett, S.-A., & Pittaway, L. (2012). Entrepreneurship education and context. *Entrepreneurship & Regional Development, 24*(9–10), 733–740.

Löbler, H. (2006). Learning entrepreneurship from a constructivist perspective. *Technology Analysis & Strategic Management, 18*(1), 19–38.

Marsick V. J. & O'Neil, J. (1999). The many faces of action learning. *Management Learning, 30*(2), 159–176.

McLellan, J. A., & Dewey, J. (1889). *Applied psychology: an introduction to the principles and practice of education.* Boston: Copp, Clark.

Mezirow, J. (1991). *Transformative dimensions of adult learning.* San Francisco: Jossey-Bass.

Minniti, M., & Bygrave, W. (2001). A dynamic model of entrepreneurial learning. *Entrepreneurship Theory & Practice, 25*(3), 5–16.

Mueller, S., & Anderson, A. R. (2014). Understanding the entrepreneurial learning process and its impact on students' personal development: a European perspective. *The International Journal of Management Education, 12*(3), 500–511.

Neck, H. M., & Corbett, A. C. (2018). The scholarship of teaching and learning entrepreneurship. *Entrepreneurship Education & Pedagogy, 1*(1), 8–41.

Neck, H. M., & Greene, P. G. (2011). Entrepreneurship education: known worlds and new frontiers. *Journal of Small Business Management, 49*(1), 55–70.

Neck, H. M., Greene, P. G., & Brush, C. G. (2014). *Teaching entrepreneurship: A practice-based approach.* Cheltenham, UK: Edward Elgar.

Neufeld, V. R., & Barrows, H. S. (1974). The" McMaster Philosophy": an approach to medical education. *Academic Medicine, 49*(11), 1040–1050.

Pedler, M., Burgoyne, J., & Brook, C. (2005). What has action learning learned to become? *Action Learning, 2*(1), 49–68.

Pittaway, L., & Cope, J. (2007). Entrepreneurship education a systematic review of the evidence. *International Small Business Journal, 25*(5), 479–510.

Pittaway, L., Missing, C., Hudson, N., & Maragh, D. (2009). Entrepreneurial learning through action: a case study of the Six-Squared program. *Action Learning: Research and Practice, 6*(3), 265–288.

Politis, D. (2005a). *Entrepreneurship, career experience and learning-developing our understanding of entrepreneurship as an experiential learning process.* Compilation, Lund University, Lund: MediaTryck.

Politis, D. (2005b). The process of entrepreneurial learning: a conceptual framework. *Entrepreneurship Theory and Practice, 29*(4), 399–424.

Rae, D., & Carswell, M. (2001). Towards a conceptual understanding of entrepreneurial learning. *Journal of Small Business and Enterprise Development, 8*(2), 150–158.

Rae, D. (2009). Connecting entrepreneurial and action learning in student-initiated new business ventures: the case of SPEED. *Action Learning: Research and Practice, 6*(3), 289–303.

Rasmussen, E. A., & Sørheim, R. (2006). Action-based entrepreneurship education. *Technovation, 26*(2), 185–194.

Revans, R. W. (1982). What is action learning? *Journal of Management Development, 1*(3), 64–75.

Revans, R. W. (2011). *ABC of action learning.* Farnham, England: Gower Publishing Ltd.

Roberts, J. W. (2012). *Beyond learning by doing: theoretical currents in experiential education.* New York: Routledge.

Robinson, S., Neergaard, H., Tanggaard, L., & Krueger, N. (2016). New horizons in entrepreneurship: from teacher-led to student-centered learning. *Education + Training, 58*(7/8), 661–683.

Ronstadt, R. (1985). The educated entrepreneurs: a new era of entrepreneurial education is beginning. *American Journal of Small Business, 10*(1), 7–23.

San Tan, S., & Ng, C. F. (2006). A problem-based learning approach to entrepreneurship education. *Education + Training, 48*(6), 416–428.

Sarasvathy, S. D., & Venkataraman, S. (2011). Entrepreneurship as method: open questions for an entrepreneurial future. *Entrepreneurship Theory & Practice, 35*(1), 113–135.

Savery, J. R. (2006). Overview of problem-based learning: definitions and distinctions. *Interdisciplinary Journal of Problem-based Learning, 1*(1), 9–20.

Schmidt, H. G. (1993). Foundations of problem-based learning: some explanatory notes. *Medical Education, 27*(5), 422–432.

Sexton, D. L., & Bowman-Upton, N. (1987). Evaluation of an innovative approach to teaching entrepreneurship. *Journal of Small Business Management, 25*(1), 35–43.

Solomon, G. T., Weaver, K. M., & Fernald, L. W. (1994). A historical examination of small business management and entrepreneurship pedagogy. *Simulation & Gaming, 25*(3), 338–352.

Sweller, J. (2015). In Academe, What is learned, and how is it learned? *Current Directions in Psychological Science, 24*(3), 190–194.

Sweller, J., Ayres, P., & Kalyuga, S. (2011). *Cognitive load theory.* New York: Springer.

Sweller, J., Kirschner, P. A., & Clark, R. E. (2007). Why minimally guided teaching techniques do not work: A reply to commentaries. *Educational Psychologist, 42*(2), 115–121.

Thomassen, M. L., Middleton, K. W., Ramsgaard, M. B., Neergaard, H., & Warren, L. (2019). Conceptualizing context in entrepreneurship education: a literature review. *International Journal of Entrepreneurial Behavior & Research*, 26(5), 863–886.

Thomson, J. A. K., Tredennick, H., & Barnes, J. (2004). *Aristotle – the Nicomachean ethics.* London: Penguin Books.

Wee, K. N. L. (2004). A problem-based learning approach in entrepreneurship education: promoting authentic entrepreneurial learning. *International Journal of Technology Management, 28*(7), 685–701.

Welsh, D. H., Tullar, W. L., & Nemati, H. (2016). Entrepreneurship education: process, method, or both? *Journal of Innovation & Knowledge, 1*(3), 125–132.

Welter, F. (2011). Contextualizing entrepreneurship – conceptual challenges and ways forward. *Entrepreneurship Theory & Practice, 35*(1), 165–184.

3 Trends in the Development of Entrepreneurial Education as a Research Field (1980–2018)

3.1 Looking Back to Gaze Ahead

The field of entrepreneurial education has seen tremendous progress over the last four decades since becoming established in higher education. The development can be seen both in the interest of policy makers addressed in Chapter 1 as well as in relation to pedagogical and andragogical development as discussed in Chapter 2. The community of scholars has also developed with the emergence of specialized conferences together with the increased number of outlets dedicated to publishing scholarly work on entrepreneurial education, such as *Education + Training* (annual double special issues) and the recently launched *Entrepreneurship Education & Pedagogy* journal as well as special issues in some of the main entrepreneurship journals. All these initiatives have provided a broad platform for developing and growing the field of research. Given this expansion and the continuous arguments for taking stock of how the field is maturing and whether it has started to gain legitimacy, the following empirical chapter descriptively discusses the development of the field. It does so by making use of a systematic literature review methodology comprising 447 articles published between 1980 and the end of 2018. Previous research has acknowledged that there is little theoretical and methodological development (Fayolle, 2013; Rideout & Gray, 2013) and that the field in general is searching for legitimacy (Fayolle, Verzat, & Wapshott, 2016). However, there are also recent reviews arguing that entrepreneurial education has started to develop as a distinct field (Gabrielsson, Hägg, Landström, & Politis, 2020). In the following sections we address this issue and investigate the development to date. Before presenting the empirical insights from the Systematic Literature Review (SLR), we discuss the method used to collect the 447 articles that make up the empirical material for the continuing discussion.

DOI: 10.4324/9781003194972-3

3.2 Research Design and Method

The research design builds upon the recent studies published by Hägg and Gabrielsson (2019) and Gabrielsson et al. (2020), adopting systematic and bibliometric literature review methodology to develop both knowledge of the past and insights for the future. However, the present chapter and the empirical insights from the systematic literature review differ in scope. A main difference between the present chapter and the study by Hägg and Gabrielsson (2019) is the focus on aggregative patterns that emerge from the descriptive data coded on all articles included in the sample. The systematic literature review by Hägg and Gabrielsson (2019) has a configurative approach. According to Gough, Thomas and Oliver (2012), there are conceptual differences between an aggregative and a configurative SLR approach, where the configurative seeks to interpret and understand a particular phenomenon, while the aggregative collects empirical data to test and describe predefined concepts and their development. In contrast to the study by Gabrielsson et al. (2020), the present chapter makes use of the entire descriptive coding, including all 447 articles, whilst the study by Gabrielsson et al. (2020) had the full sample as an initial step for conducting a more refined bibliometric analysis than would normally be the case when using only Boolean search terms in, for example, Scopus. Hence, in comparison to the study by Hägg and Gabrielsson (2019) the present chapter has a slightly larger sample due to an increased number of search terms (from 395 to 447 articles) and focuses on the descriptively coded information from the articles (making it an aggregative SLR). In comparison to the study by Gabrielsson et al. (2020), the present chapter differs both by employing the entire sample (447 as opposed to 340 articles) as well as methodologically, as a bibliometric analysis was not conducted, and the timeline is different (38 years as opposed to 24 years).

3.2.1 Systematic Literature Review Method

The systematic literature review method builds on developing a process for identifying relevant records in a replicable and transparent way. The systematic review procedure in the present chapter follows the steps proposed by Tranfield, Denyer and Smart (2003), including (1) planning the review and setting research objectives and defining conceptual boundaries, (2) conducting the review and the systematized procedure for coding and collecting articles and (3) reporting and disseminating the outcomes.

The first step of the methodology included setting the boundaries where education was defined in a broad sense "as the action or process of facilitating learning in a formal setting under the guidance of instructors, or the knowledge and development resulting from such an educational process" (Hägg & Gabrielsson, 2019, p. 833). In addition, entrepreneurial education was employed to capture the breadth of the field and the two sub-fields of entrepreneurship and enterprise education. Given the interrelation that exists between the two terms and their history, both terms were considered equally important for systematically capturing the development of the field. After setting the boundaries a coding structure was developed that enabled the collection and standardization of information about each article, including author(s) names, the institutions and the countries where authors were affiliated, main topic area, theoretical frameworks and reference theories used, classification of research methods and summaries of main findings including the main research questions and their answers. In contrast to Hägg and Gabrielsson (2019), the present chapter uses standardized information, but does not make use of the main findings and conclusions as they have been reported previously in the configurative review by Hägg and Gabrielsson (2019).

The next step of the method includes conducting the review. To create the database only peer-reviewed papers written in English were included and we restricted the inclusion of articles from open access journals due to the issue of rating quality. The timeframe was set from 1980, as that year saw the emergence of entrepreneurship as an academic field, including the launch of the *Journal of Business Venturing* (JBV), *Entrepreneurship and Regional Development* (ERD) and the *International Small Business Journal* (ISBJ) as well as the development of the Babson conference and the RENT conference. Moreover, we used Business Source Complete (BSC) and Education Resources Information Centre (ERIC) as bibliographic databases, as they matched our demands for coverage and full article access. As addressed in Gabrielsson et al. (2020), a series of keywords were developed into Boolean search terms and entered into the databases. Keywords used in the search were: "Entrepreneurship Education" (or) "Enterprise Education" (or) "Entrepreneurial Education" (or) "Action-based Entrepreneurship Education" (or) "Practice-based Entrepreneurship Education" (or) "Action-oriented Entrepreneurship

Education" (or) "Project-based Entrepreneurship Education" (or) "Entrepreneur* Teaching" (or) "Enterprise Teaching". The search generated 1,341 hits. Of these, 934 were excluded due to not addressing either pedagogy or entrepreneurial education in substantial depth throughout the article. Following this step, a manual search was also conducted to identify other studies that could potentially fit the objectives, which resulted in 40 additional articles, yielding a final sample of 447 articles.

According to Tranfield et al. (2003), the final step of the SLR method is to report and disseminate the outcomes of the systematic search and coding. In this we followed the advice of Gough et al. (2012), where we analysed the descriptive data using an aggregative approach. This means that in the following sections we discuss the development of the field with regard to its growth over time, the contextual development related to scholars and their collaboration over various boundaries (co-authorship, cross-institutional, national and continental). This is then followed by an analysis of the empirical context such as geographical scope and educational setting of the research that has been foundational in the development of the field of entrepreneurial education. Following this we analyse the research focus that includes theoretical approaches, main research question (focus on student learning, assessment, evaluation etc.) and type of study (conceptual or empirical). Finally, the last part of this chapter analyses the methodological development that addresses qualitative versus quantitative studies and the various methods used in each area. The chapter ends with a short conclusion on what the data has revealed regarding trends.

3.3 The Basic Dynamics of the Field

In this chapter we analyse and summarize the data illustrating the basic dynamics of entrepreneurial education as a research field departing from the questions addressed in the introduction:

1. What developmental trends can we see regarding theoretical and methodological advancement in studies on entrepreneurship and enterprising education?
2. What trends can be seen in the development of entrepreneurship and enterprising education in regard to contextual lenses related to the community development?

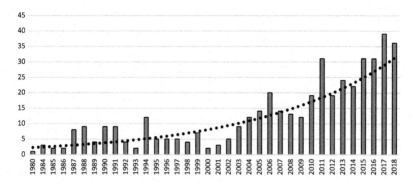

Figure 3.1 Number of papers per year.

3.3.1 The Aggregate View of the Sample

Number of papers. The bar chart in Figure 3.1 illustrates the number of papers on entrepreneurial education between 1980 and 2018. The following analysis involves 447 published papers, the main scope of which is entrepreneurial education as revealed in our search based on the selection criterion described above. The database opens with an article by Clarke and Reavley on "Educating Technical Entrepreneurs and Innovators for the 1980's" published in *Technovation*. Given the fact that entrepreneurship was recognized as a driver of job creation and the political push it received, the 1980s was nevertheless still at an infant stage of development with less journal publications, which is also evident in the development of the field.

The initial two decades were largely driven by individual pioneers as in the case of the establishment of entrepreneurship as a domain (see Landström, 2010), including prominent scholars such as Karl Vesper, Ed McMullan, Wayne Long, Donald Sexton and Nancy Bowman in North America and Allan Gibb in the UK to mention just a few. They were followed by additional influential scholars in the 1990s such as George Solomon, Jerome Katz, Jean-Pierre Béchard and Jean-Marie Toulouse and Robert Brockhaus, who in the 1991 paper acknowledged a context beyond that of the Western industrialized world. Although plenty of individual contributions have been key to the development of the field worldwide, there is not sufficient space to acknowledge all of them, but without the collective effort that has driven the multiple conversations, the field or research area that we know today as entrepreneurship, enterprise and entrepreneurial education would not be as rich. Given the global reach that we can see today and the impact that entrepreneurial education has in all parts of the world (Morris & Liguori, 2016), it is important to address how these scholarly efforts have shaped the field. Over the last four decades we can see an evolutionary increase in published articles from just one paper in 1980 to 36 papers in 2018. By evolutionary we mean that the growth is not on a continuous, year-by-year basis, but an overall progression can be seen if we look at Figure 3.1. In Figure 3.1 we can observe an upward trend in the publication of articles on entrepreneurial education, which might be interpreted as a sign of a growing interest in the topic on the part of researchers, as well as an increasing interest of journal editors to publish papers on entrepreneurial education. However, as addressed in Chapter 1, special issues have created some of the peaks in the early development of the field, whilst the last decade or so has led to a steadier development, where the infrastructure of regular double special issues in *Education + Training* as well as the launch of field-specific journals has created an arena for scholars to discuss key issues. The scope of where scholars in entrepreneurial education publish is important for understanding the arena and also the potential for joining the various discussions in the field. Therefore, the following section addresses how various journal outlets have played a role over time.

Entrepreneurial Education Journals. An interest in entrepreneurship and small business developed during the 1970s, while an interest in educating within the topics developed in the 1980s. Given the ties to entrepreneurship and small business, the early contributions in the 1980s and 1990s are mainly found in field-specific journals as well as journals that addressed methods of instruction, such as simulations (see also Gabrielsson et al., 2020). However, the early connections to entrepreneurship and small business regarding journal outlets have diminished in scope and today it is more likely to find scholarly discussions on entrepreneurial education in the field-specific journal *Entrepreneurship Education and Pedagogy* (launched in 2018) as well as in vocational training-oriented journals such as *Education + Training* as well as *Industry and Higher Education*. On the aggregate level of the sample, we find two European journals, *Education + Training* (116 papers) and *Industry and Higher Education* (48 papers). Other journals that have played a role in the dissemination of entrepreneurial education research are the *Journal of Entrepreneurship*

Education (22 papers), *Journal of Small Business Management* (21 papers), as well as one of the leading outlets in entrepreneurship – the *Journal of Business Venturing* (15 papers). However, when looking more closely at the sample of articles, it should be noted that different decades were characterized by various temporal trends. For example, *Simulation and Gaming* was a popular outlet for entrepreneurial education scholars in the 1990s with 12 papers published between 1994 and 1999, but has since largely disappeared as a platform for further discussion. As stated at the beginning of the section, the influence of field-specific journals on entrepreneurship and small business has decreased, but there is still a number of journals such as the *Journal of Small Business Management*, the *International Small Business Journal* and the *International Journal of Entrepreneurial Behaviour and Research* that continuously provide opportunities for scholars to report important insights pertaining to entrepreneurial education. However, the top journals in entrepreneurship *(Journal of Business Venturing and Entrepreneurship Theory & Practice)* were far more influential in the early stage and despite making room for a handful of papers over the last two decades, all of which received a fair number of citations and also impacted the field (see also Gabrielsson et al., 2020), the main conversations regarding conceptual development and empirical research are much more tied to field-specific journals and journals more closely associated with education and vocational and work-based learning. To conclude this first aggregate analysis, there is a trend towards finding a specific arena where the scholarly discussion can take place and it also provides a fertile ground for the broadening of what entrepreneurial education might mean, as it is not only tied to the narrow view of how to start and manage a business but also includes the educational side of how to teach, what to teach and which audience we are targeting. In this sense the discussion is much broader than the scope that might be seen as relevant in field-specific journals such as *Entrepreneurship Theory & Practice* and the *Journal of Business Venturing*.

3.4 The Context of Research in Entrepreneurial Education

3.4.1 The Context of Academic Cooperation

To address the context, in this first section we will discuss how the academic discussion has evolved when it comes to cooperation. The context of academic cooperation is described by considering four aspects: co-authorship of papers, cross-university, cross-country and

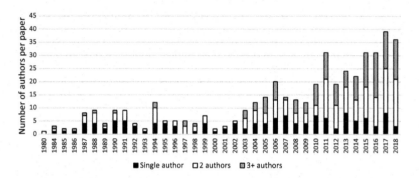

Figure 3.2 Co-authorship.

cross-continental cooperation between authors publishing on entrepreneurial education.

Co-authorship. The bar chart in Figure 3.2 provides an illustrative view of how the papers on entrepreneurial education put forward single author ideas or cooperation among scholars. We divided the population of papers into three groups: single-authored, with two authors, and with three or more authors. In total, in the period under investigation, 129 papers were written by sole authors, 177 papers by two authors and 141 papers by three or more authors. However, whereas the number of single-authored papers fluctuates over time without a dominant tendency, co-authorship is clearly gaining popularity, especially multiple (3+) authored papers. This trend of increased co-authorship is most notable in the last decade of the analysed period. There are two potential explanations for this increasing trend of multiple authored papers. Firstly, there is a growing community and platform where scholars in the field can meet, interact and develop collaboration to conduct studies, as well as the closeness that digitalization has brought. In addition, the advancement of the field also leads to the demand for interdisciplinary expertise, which is easier to fulfil in situations where there is more than one author. A second potential explanation has more to do with a publish and perish paradigm that has developed, where scholars are forced to continuously produce and publish scholarly work to move up the ladder. However, there is still a fair amount of heterogeneity where individual scholars provide their insights and collaborative authorship is evident.

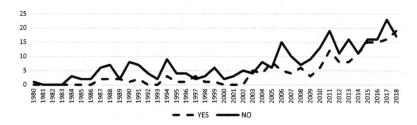

Figure 3.3 Cross-HEI cooperation.

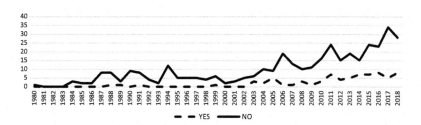

Figure 3.4 Cross-country cooperation.

Scope of collaboration. When moving forward to scope of collaboration, we address how much variation there is in relation to within as well as between university collaboration. Out of 447 papers, 164 papers were published as a result of cross-HEI collaboration (283 without it), 74 papers as cross-country collaboration (373 without it) and only 40 papers with cross-continent collaboration (407 without it). Beginning with Figure 3.3, we see the development of collaboration between universities in a single country. As the field has developed through pioneers in different countries, for example, in Canada with the work of Ed McMullen and colleagues at the university of Calgary, progress has been rather slow in generating within country collaboration. As we can see from Figure 3.4, cross-country collaboration is even less developed. Out of the 447 papers a mere 16.5 percent of the scholarly publications actually goes beyond the national context for understanding and discussing the phenomenon. If we then move to cross-continent collaboration, as seen in Figure 3.5, we can see an even lower number of scholarly works with collaboration between continents. Of the entire sample, only 9 percent was the result of cross-continent collaboration among the authors.

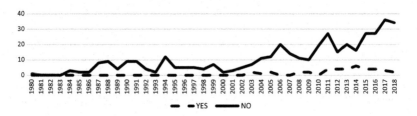

Figure 3.5 Cross-continent cooperation.

Given that the vast majority of studies are developed within a very specific context, it could be argued that over the years many perspectives have portrayed what should be taught, how it should be taught and why it should be taught. Cultural and contextual factors have played a role in developing various insights, which could explain some of the discussions that are taking place in the field and why there are questions around legitimacy and maturity (e.g., Fayolle et al., 2016; Jones & Iredale, 2010; Neck & Corbett, 2018). However, a positive trend that can be seen in Figures 3.3–3.5 is that some changes have taken place in the last 15 years. Although the lack of cross-HEI cooperation is dominant in most of the years analysed, the share of papers written in cross-HEI collaboration is growing, albeit not in a systematic manner. If we compare the first 20 years of analysis with the last 18 years, the share of cross-HEI papers increased twofold, from about 21 percent to 41 percent. Cross-country cooperation is weaker. During the 1980s and 1990s, there were only 4 papers published by co-authors representing different countries (in comparison with 87 published by solo authors and in-country teams). The next two decades brought some change, as between 2000 and 2018, 70 out of 356 papers (20 percent) were published by co-authors from different countries. Cross-continent cooperation did not start until 2003 and so far is developing rather slowly. Although the number of papers with cross-continent cooperation has grown slightly in recent years, the number of papers without it is growing even faster. Therefore, despite some signs of international cooperation, research in entrepreneurial education remains fairly local in terms of author affiliation.

3.4.2 The Empirical Context of Studies

The context of the research in entrepreneurial education refers not only to academic cooperation but also to the empirical context of studies.

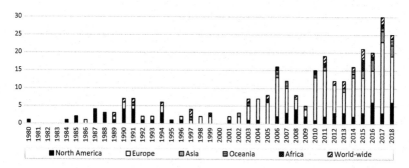

Figure 3.6 Empirical context – continent.

Figure 3.7 Empirical context – North America versus Europe.

In this case, it is interesting to know whether the empirics are of cross-continent or cross-country coverage or based on more national or local data, as well as what kind of educational setting they relate to.

Empirical context in geographical terms. Between 1980 and 2018, most of the empirical papers in entrepreneurial education referred to Europe (159) and North America (70), and much less to Asia (16), Oceania (12) and Africa (10). There were also 22 studies in a world context but none with a context exclusively in South America. The bar chart in Figure 3.6 presents the distribution of a continental context of papers in the analysed timeframe. Throughout the period, the dominance of Europe and North America as research contexts is very clear, but their prevalence also increased over time. If we look more closely at the dynamics in a number of papers and compare their empirical context – Europe versus North America (Figure 3.7) – it is evident that in the first two decades, i.e., between 1980 and 1999, North America (the US and Canada) to a large extent determined the empirical context in entrepreneurial education (27 papers as opposed to 15 referring to the European context), whereas in the next two decades, i.e., between 2000 and 2018, Europe was definitely more often selected as an empirical setting (144 papers as opposed to 43 referring to the North American context). In particular, the last ten years have deepened the divergence. When the comparison is completed on a country level, the empirical contexts in entrepreneurial education papers are mainly related to the UK, the US, Sweden, Australia and Canada. Therefore, the Anglo-Saxon view on education remains dominant and, in some way, influences the global view of entrepreneurial education. However, given the criteria of the review method of including only peer-reviewed papers as well as those written in the English language, it is most likely that our sample does not touch upon parallel streams of research that have influenced national and continental development. Furthermore, we do not consider conference papers or grey literature (e.g., policy reports) in this chapter; thus our trends and arguments should be reflected upon on the basis of peer-reviewed English language journal publications. The analysis of the empirical context of papers in entrepreneurial education may be seen as confirmation of the claims of Henrich, Heine and Norenzayan (2010) that leading journals publish papers based on samples drawn from Western, Educated, Industrialized, Rich and Democratic (WEIRD) societies. However, from the late 1990s, the discussion opens up for more diversity in terms of the origin of empirical context. Moreover, the European view is not homogenous as it is not only developed in the UK, and thus the Scandinavian school as well as the

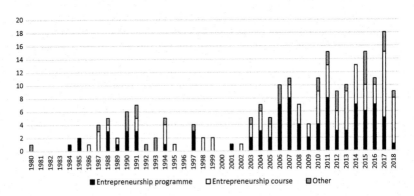

Figure 3.8 Empirical context – educational setting.

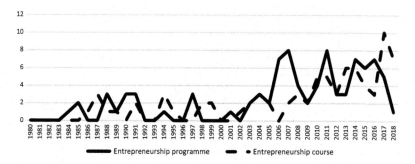

Figure 3.9 Empirical context – entrepreneurship programme versus entrepreneurship course.

French contributions, in particular from Alain Fayolle and colleagues, should also be taken into account.

In our analysis, we also included the educational setting of the empirical context and differentiated between entrepreneurship programme, entrepreneurship course and other type of setting (Figures 3.8 and 3.9). In total, between 1980 and 2018, among the 208 investigated empirical papers on entrepreneurial education with a given educational setting, 43 percent related to an entrepreneurship programme, 39 percent to an entrepreneurship course and 18 percent to other types of setting. Interestingly, the division of papers relating to entrepreneurship programmes and entrepreneurship courses in the 1980s and 1990s is almost identical to the next two decades. Between 1980 and 1999, the share was 52 percent and 48 percent, whereas between 2000 and 2018 it was 53 percent and 47 percent respectively. Therefore, there is a steady and equal interest in these two types of educational setting.

3.5 Development of Research Focus in Entrepreneurial Education

Grasping the development of entrepreneurial education as a field of research also requires a more detailed analysis regarding changes in research focus as applied in the papers. In this study, we decided to follow it from three perspectives. Firstly, we discuss the theoretical approach, where we divide papers into four groups: those with a clear theory development (labelled theory driven), those drawing from a mix of theories and at least partly contributing to theoretical aspects

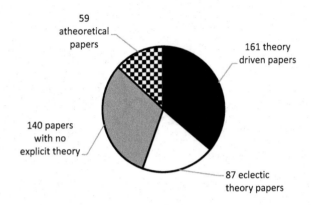

Figure 3.10 Theoretical approach (1980–2018).

(labelled eclectic), papers not referring to a particular theory but with a substantive number of references to the literature (labelled no explicit theory) and papers where any theoretical discussion is absent and the literature grounding of the study is marginal or non-existent (labelled atheoretical). The second perspective relates to the main focus of the papers, which reflects the chief research problem or research question. In this analysis, we group papers into five categories: (1) those referring to the programme/course design, (2) concentrated on student learning, (3) aimed at different types of evaluation, (4) policy papers and (5) others. Finally, the third perspective is linked to the type of study, whether the papers are conceptual, empirical or take the form of a review. In each perspective we tried to present the overall structure of the research focus, as well as the dynamics of different types of papers over time.

Theoretical approach. The analysis of a theoretical approach leads to a rather optimistic picture of the field. Between 1980 and 2018, out of 447 papers, 161 were theory driven, 87 eclectic, 140 had no explicit theory and 59 were atheoretical (Figure 3.10).

Importantly, the number of theory-driven papers is growing (Figure 3.11). The growth of theory-driven papers is particularly evident in the last decade of the analysis, where they account for 43 percent of all papers published. At the same time, the share of atheoretical papers is decreasing (Figure 3.12), which also provides some initial insights that the field is at least moving in the direction of gaining maturity, where it is no longer possible to get papers with only inductively driven ideas published as the scholarly knowledge has increased. In the last decade

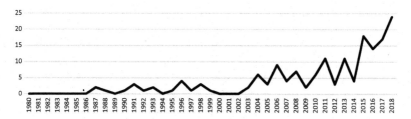

Figure 3.11 Theory-driven papers.

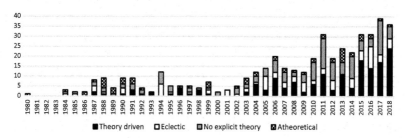

■ Theory driven   □ Eclectic   ◫ No explicit theory   ▨ Atheoretical

Figure 3.12 Theoretical approach.

the number of atheoretical papers declined to 9 percent. More alarming could be the still relatively high ratio of papers with no explicit theory, as in the last decade it reached 32.5 percent. This could be explained by the coding premise of the analysis, which does not capture the more empirically driven pedagogical discussion that takes place in many of the empirical studies. However, as a scholarly field there has to be more theoretical anchoring when conducting empirical studies. This recognition follows the insights presented by Rideout and Gray (2013) as well as arguments made by Fayolle et al. (2016) and insights addressed by Pittaway and Cope (2007). However, the ongoing discussion on being close to practice and not residing in only introverted academic discussions and the nature of the empirical phenomenon also give some hints as to why less theory-driven papers still have a place in the discussion.

Focus of papers. When we go further into the coding and examine the research focus of the papers, the total sample is divided into 149 papers related to student learning, 133 papers to evaluation, 98 papers to programme/course design, whilst only 18 are policy papers and 49 papers do not belong to any of these categories (Figure 3.13). From an

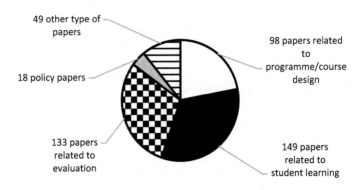

49 other type of papers

18 policy papers

133 papers related to evaluation

98 papers related to programme/course design

149 papers related to student learning

Figure 3.13 Focus of the paper (1980–2018).

overall viewpoint there seems to be a fairly balanced mix of studies that covers much of the field and the different parts that could be argued to play a role in its development. However, as the field has been pushed forward by policy and many political arguments that society needs more entrepreneurially talented citizens (as addressed in Chapter 1), it is quite interesting to note that the political side has evoked only modest interest. This might also be due to the focus of the systematic literature review search adopted and that much of the discussion regarding policy is found in other forms of scholarly investigation that are not peer-reviewed articles. This could also be because there has been less attention to policy as the main focus has been on addressing what is actually going on in the classroom. An additional issue is that the field is rather young and taking on policy perspectives might not be as high on the agenda in the early phases as the primary interest lies in understanding the phenomenon and developing the infrastructure and some basic common ground on what the foundations of the field as a scholarly domain might be (see Landström, 2020 for a discussion on development of scholarly fields). Another issue is that the last category does not specifically reside in any of the first four groups. The 49 papers in the other focus category either develop their discussion on why enterprise or entrepreneurship is different from management or how practitioners are of importance for entrepreneurial education, as well as more aggregate discussions such as the role of philosophy in entrepreneurial education. This group of papers touches upon student learning and programme design or evaluation, but does not have a specific focus on either of these areas.

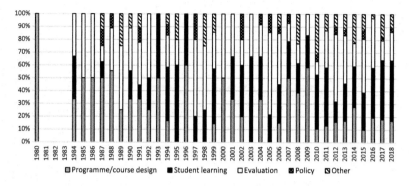

Figure 3.14 Focus of the paper.

When we break our sample down into year by year and look at the trend over time, we can see that there is a rise in popularity of the first two groups of papers, namely evaluation and student learning. This is particularly evident in the last decade of the analysis (Figure 3.14). At the same time, the interest in the topic of programme/course design is decreasing after having received a great deal of attention up until 2010. The share of papers with a focus on programme/course design reached 48 percent in the first decade of analysis, in the second decade 23 percent, in the third 28 percent and only 16 percent during the last decade up until the end of 2018. There seems to be a trend towards a focus on the learning process and evaluations of that process, which agrees with previous claims about the development made by Hägg and Gabrielsson (2019). A main difference here is that the aforementioned study addressed the patterns of what was concluded in the different studies, whilst the present analysis looks at the aggregate focus areas. However, there is an alignment in the view that student learning is a key that is then further addressed by seeking to understand how to actually evaluate this learning on group and individual level.

Type of study. As a final part of understanding the development of research focus in the field, we address what types of study are published over time. In this we distinguished between conceptual and empirical studies and found that the most frequently published papers are empirical, which amount to 62 percent (278 papers), in comparison to conceptual papers that account for 29 percent (129) and reviews that amount to 9 percent (40) of the full sample. We find that not only has the number

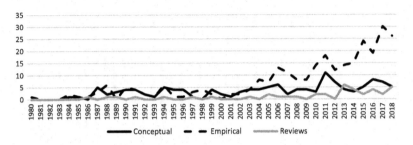

Figure 3.15 Type of study.

of empirical papers continued to grow over time but also their overall share of the total number of publications. Given that we noticed a theoretical development in section 3.4 of this chapter, it could be a sign that the threshold for publishing conceptual papers is becoming higher as the field matures. Also, that there is a greater need for empirical studies that seek to test and further develop the existing conceptual models and frameworks.

As illustrated in Figure 3.15, somewhere around the middle of the period under investigation, there is a breakdown of the slight domination of conceptual papers in favour of empirical ones. The number of reviews is still marginal but has also grown slightly in the last ten years. As the field is growing and the number of published papers in various sub-areas related to entrepreneurial education is increasing, there is also currently a more pressing need for good review papers that can take stock of the knowledge development over time and specific topics that are important for the aggregate understanding of the field (see Bae, Qian, Miao, & Fiet, 2014; Blenker, Elmholdt, Frederiksen, Korsgaard, & Wagner, 2014; Henry & Lewis, 2018; Nabi, Liñán, Fayolle, Krueger, & Walmsley, 2017).

3.6 Methodological Development of the Field

As a final part of our coding of the sample we examine the methodological development of entrepreneurial education as a research field. In this section we are interested in the data collection approach applied in empirical papers, i.e., whether studies were quantitative, qualitative or if authors used a mix of quantitative and qualitative methods. The mixed method approach has been highly argued for to create justification and rigour in entrepreneurship studies at large (Molina-Azorín,

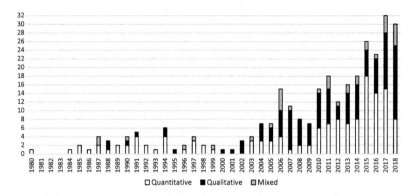

Figure 3.16 Data collection approach.

López-Gamero, Pereira-Moliner, & Pertusa-Ortega, 2012), as well as in entrepreneurial education studies (Blenker et al., 2014). We deepened our analysis by also discussing the source of data collection. Among quantitative papers, we differentiated between papers using archival data, those relying on questionnaires, those with mixed methods of obtaining data and others. Qualitative papers were grouped into those that build their methodology based on observations, interviews, panel/focus group discussions, secondary data, reflections and mixed methods.

Data collection approach. Out of a total of 300 empirical papers (empirical papers and empirical reviews with a clearly stated method of data collection) published between 1980 and 2018, 141 are quantitative in nature, 123 are qualitative and in 36 a mix of quantitative and qualitative methods was applied (Figure 3.16). Although the argument for more mixed method papers exists and could generate more rigour of the findings, there is still little progress when it comes to this type of study. It might be that the insights such studies could bring to the field are far superior than only adopting one methodological lens as argued by Blenker et al. (2014). However, it is still troublesome to conduct such studies as they require more data and empirical material. The mixed method study also increases the length, creating problems making it difficult to adhere to the journals' word limits, and when using multiple streams of data there are higher degrees of uncertainty that there will actually be an alignment leading to new insights for the field. As seen in Figure 3.16, the use of mixed methods is fairly limited and does

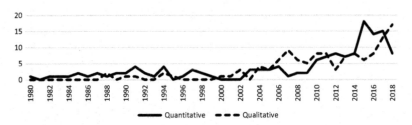

Figure 3.17 Quantitative versus qualitative approach.

not really show a progressive development in comparison to the use of qualitative methods.

If we move forward to Figure 3.17, we pay closer attention to the dynamics and development of the quantitative and qualitative methods used in studies on entrepreneurial education. During first two decades, quantitative papers outnumbered qualitative ones, where the use of surveys to find out what faculty taught or which literature that was used stood out in the early phase. However, the situation has changed in the third decade where the qualitative approach gained in popularity and dominated at the expense of the quantitative approach. The fourth decade of the analysis showed a return to the dominance of quantitative papers, which might be a sign of a more mature field as the number of qualitative studies dominated in the middle of our timeline and created a foundation to conduct more quantitative studies. Nevertheless, the share of qualitative papers in relation to quantitative papers is as high as 46.5 percent. The high number of qualitative studies in entrepreneurial education therefore contradicts the popular view among entrepreneurship scholars that qualitative approaches are deemed less acceptable by scientific journals, as there seems to be a difference in acceptance of qualitative studies in the journals that publish on entrepreneurial education. Both quantitative and qualitative methods are developing in parallel and there is a research space for both, which can be interpreted as a sign of methodological harmony in the field.

Quantitative methods. When we look into the different methods, we find that 177 papers use quantitative methods from the pool of empirical papers and reviews (both as a sole method and in papers with a mixed methodology). The most frequently used source of data was questionnaires, which were used in 131 papers, whereas the next most popular source of data – archival data was used only 31 times (Figure 3.18). Moreover, the distance between these two sources of data is growing over time.

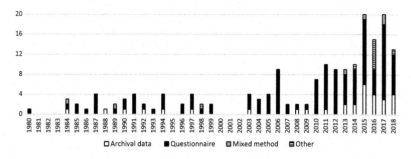

Figure 3.18 Data collection approach – quantitative studies.

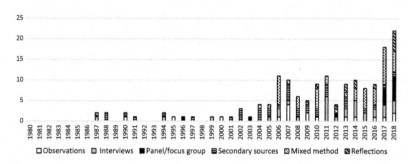

Figure 3.19 Data collection approach – qualitative studies.

This is an interesting finding, as it shows that entrepreneurial education scholars base their work on self-collected data, which demands more time and engagement, which in turn may influence the publishing process. It might also be that given the population studied (students), the use of questionnaires to grasp the learning process is preferable as there is a close connection between the teacher (often the researcher) and the students (population), which might increase the response rate but also generate biases that have to be addressed and reflected on.

Qualitative methods. Finally, in the more in-depth analysis of the qualitative methods used, we find 159 papers (both as a sole method and in papers with a mixed methodology). In the case of a qualitative approach, the division between particular sources of data is more equal (Figure 3.19). Researchers most frequently collect data by applying mixed tools (48 papers between 1980 and 2018) and by using secondary data (36 papers). Subsequently, the tools employed are interviews (31 papers), observations (17 papers), reflections (14 papers) and panel/

focus group discussions (13 papers). With regard to trends over time, the number of papers trying to apply more than one tool to obtain data is growing, which may be the sign of increased research competences on the part of scholars and a strive for a methodological soundness in the research. To reconnect back with the overarching discussion on methods, there is no general trend of adopting a mixed method approach when it comes to quantitative and qualitative methods, but within the area of qualitative methods there is a more progressive development of using several different empirical sources to gain a deeper understanding.

3.7 What Trends Are Starting to Emerge?

Building on the synthesized insights from the streams of analysis made in this chapter we can conclude that the field of entrepreneurial education, including both enterprise and entrepreneurship, has evolved and generated methodological, practical and theoretical advances but also created increased debates within and between the various sub-discussions. Through the different layers of analysis presented in this chapter we can acknowledge an increased breadth and scope of what it might imply to educate entrepreneurs and/or enterprising students in different contexts. There is a slight developmental trend when it comes to rigour in both theory and methodological harmony, but the relevance is still very much local and there is less signs of an aggregate development where multi-context studies could create broader views on where the field is heading. From the present chapter we can acknowledge that there is a theoretical development, the field has moved forward in acknowledging the importance of methodological harmony and we have noted some small steps towards cross-collaboration. However, to fully embrace and understand how these differences could further progress the field, many discussions and insights still need to be addressed. In the following chapter we will try to both synthesize what the analysis has brought and problematize some of the trends that are not evolving at a pace that could have been anticipated, given the various calls to action from scholars in the field over the decades (see, e.g., Béchard & Toulouse, 1991; Blenker et al., 2014; Fayolle, 2013; Hytti & O'Gorman, 2004; Neck & Corbett, 2018; Pittaway & Cope, 2007).

References

Bae, T. J., Qian, S., Miao, C., & Fiet, J. O. (2014). The relationship between entrepreneurship education and entrepreneurial intentions: a meta-analytic review. *Entrepreneurship Theory & Practice, 38*(2), 217–254.

Béchard, J.-P., & Toulouse, J.-M. (1991). Entrepreneurship and education: viewpoint from education. *Journal of Small Business & Entrepreneurship, 9*(1), 3–13.

Blenker, P., Elmholdt, S. T., Frederiksen, S. H., Korsgaard, S., & Wagner, K. (2014). Methods in entrepreneurship education research: a review and integrative framework. *Education + Training, 56*(8/9), 697–715.

Fayolle, A. (2013). Personal views on the future of entrepreneurship education. *Entrepreneurship & Regional Development, 25*(7–8), 692–701.

Fayolle, A., Verzat, C., & Wapshott, R. (2016). In quest of legitimacy: the theoretical and methodological foundations of entrepreneurship education research. *International Small Business Journal, 34*(7), 895–904.

Gabrielsson, J., Hägg, G., Landström, H., & Politis, D. (2020). Connecting the past with the present: the development of research on pedagogy in entrepreneurial education. *Education + Training, 62*(9), 1061–1086.

Gough, D., Thomas, J., & Oliver, S. (2012). Clarifying differences between review designs and methods. *Systematic Reviews, 1*(1), 28.

Hägg, G., & Gabrielsson, J. (2019). A systematic literature review of the evolution of pedagogy in entrepreneurial education research. *International Journal of Entrepreneurial Behavior & Research, 26*(5), 829–861.

Henrich, J., Heine, S. J., & Norenzayan, A. (2010). The weirdest people in the world? *Behavioral and Brain Sciences, 33*(2–3), 61–83.

Henry, C., & Lewis, K. (2018). A review of entrepreneurship education research: exploring the contribution of the *Education + Training* special issues. *Education + Training, 60*(3), 263–286.

Hytti, U., & O'Gorman, C. (2004). What is 'enterprise education'? An analysis of the objectives and methods of enterprise education programmes in four European countries. *Education+ Training, 46*(1), 11–23.

Jones, B., & Iredale, N. (2010). Enterprise education as pedagogy. *Education + Training, 52*(1), 7–19.

Landström, H. (2010). *Pioneers in entrepreneurship and small business research* (Vol. 8). US: Springer.

Landström, H. (2020). The evolution of entrepreneurship as a scholarly field. *Foundations and Trends in Entrepreneurship, 16*(2), 65–243.

Molina-Azorín, J. F., López-Gamero, M. D., Pereira-Moliner, J., & Pertusa-Ortega, E. M. (2012). Mixed methods studies in entrepreneurship research: applications and contributions. *Entrepreneurship & Regional Development, 24*(5–6), 425–456.

Morris, M. H., & Liguori, E. (2016). *Annals of entrepreneurship education and pedagogy – 2016*. Cheltenham, UK: Edward Elgar.

Nabi, G., Liñán, F., Fayolle, A., Krueger, N., & Walmsley, A. (2017). The impact of entrepreneurship education in higher education: a systematic review and research agenda. *Academy of Management Learning & Education, 16*(2), 277–299.

Neck, H. M., & Corbett, A. C. (2018). The scholarship of teaching and learning entrepreneurship. *Entrepreneurship Education & Pedagogy, 1*(1), 8–41.

Pittaway, L., & Cope, J. (2007). Entrepreneurship education a systematic review of the evidence. *International Small Business Journal, 25*(5), 479–510.

Rideout, E. C., & Gray, D. O. (2013). Does entrepreneurship education really work? A review and methodological critique of the empirical literature on the effects of university-based entrepreneurship education. *Journal of Small Business Management, 51*(3), 329–351.

Tranfield, D., Denyer, D., & Smart, P. (2003). Towards a methodology for developing evidence-informed management knowledge by means of systematic review. *British Journal of Management, 14*(3), 207–222.

4 Perspectives of Entrepreneurial Education

4.1 Reviewing the State of the Art in Entrepreneurial Education Research

The aim of Chapter 3 was to determine the extent to which entrepreneurial education as a scholarly field has developed during the last four decades. The careful analysis of the dynamics of the field, its research focus and methodology demonstrate that entrepreneurial education has come a long way from the initial and very sporadic papers in the 1980s towards more regular and rigorous publications today.

In general, the last four decades has been a time of positive movement towards legitimization of entrepreneurial education as a research field as well as a teaching practice in higher education. Paradoxically, as described in Chapter 1, academic acceptance has been more acknowledged and achieved in education practice, as courses in entrepreneurship have spread relatively quickly in HEI all over the world. The practical nature and experiential character of how entrepreneurs exploit opportunities also paved the way for experimentation with pedagogical methods, which became a fertile ground for researching what works and what does not work (teaching and research are often performed by the same group of individuals). The development of the field was inspired by mainstream entrepreneurship and its progress has resulted in continuous adjustments to curricula and new teaching challenges in entrepreneurial education. The inflow of ideas from how entrepreneurs and small business owners learn, together with an early interest in experimentation, have created a very dynamic and to some extent uncertain environment when seeking to build legitimacy for entrepreneurial education and further advancement where experimentation and co-creation have been central. Although the field of general education, with a sound theoretical grounding and rich tradition of research practice, was at arm's length, entrepreneurial education instead tried

DOI: 10.4324/9781003194972-4

to pave the way itself, from the beginning manifesting its independence and specificity in terms of learning approaches and teaching methods (Sexton & Bowman, 1984; Sexton & Bowman-Upton, 1987). From the outset, entrepreneurial education identified itself as a sub-field of entrepreneurship, not as a potential sub-field of general education, where the idea of facing uncertainty has been proclaimed as a way to become entrepreneurial (Kyrö, 2015).

The self-selected identity is very meaningful for the profile and dynamics of the field, but results in both positive and negative consequences. The strive for separation from general education potentially leads to the risk of "reinventing the wheel", where scholars have continuously called for better integration between educational science and entrepreneurship (Béchard & Toulouse, 1991; Fayolle, Verzat, & Wapshott, 2016; Pittaway & Cope, 2007). Drawing more from the well-developed discipline could speed up the maturation and advancement of entrepreneurial education as well as increase the chance of publishing in well-established journals as theoretical and methodological maturity can be found in educational science. Venturing on an individual path of development, and somehow creating the field from the roots, was certainly a more challenging decision that demanded greater efforts from the early pioneers and communities of scholars in entrepreneurial education. Furthermore, the early call for building a strong infrastructure focused on "curriculum development, course content and problems associated with course or program development" (Sexton & Bowman, 1984, pp. 21–22). The hope is, however, that by inventing or progressively developing a separate and specific enough domain full academic legitimization will be achieved.

As also described in Chapter 1, the birth of entrepreneurial education as a research field and practice was very specific and context related. Although it was greatly supported by public policies in most developed countries, academic rigour demands both time and accumulation of integrated output. The integration of the field, development of more systematic frameworks and approaches, as well as the professional culture around the phenomenon are parts of a long-term process that cannot be rapidly achieved. The time span of four decades is adequate to verify the field's progress.

This is obviously not the first attempt to look at the field as a whole. During recent years, numerous reviews have been conducted by scholars in the field, which helped to streamline the research framework. Therefore, in our discussion on the development of the field we start by referring to the findings of others. We refer to previous studies to draw the wider picture and set the scene for a broader discussion. In particular, we relate to those review studies that we believe have greatly influenced research on entrepreneurial education and to those that are fairly recent but with a broad scope to cover the development of the field. As a result, we refer to works of Dainow (1986), Gorman, Hanlon and King (1997), Béchard and Grégoire (2005), Pittaway and Cope (2007), Mwasalwiba (2010), Fayolle (2013), Fayolle et al. (2016), Nabi, Liñán, Fayolle, Krueger and Walmsley (2017), Hägg and Gabrielsson (2019), Gabrielsson, Hägg, Landström and Politis (2020), as well as Landström, Gabrielsson, Politis, Sörheim and Djupdal (2021). We are aware that this is not an all-inclusive list of reviews on research in entrepreneurial education. They were subjectively selected taking the timespan, coverage and completeness of the reviews into account, as well as the significance and power of their findings and recommendations.

One of the first reviews of entrepreneurial education research was conducted by Dainow (1986), who ended his analysis in 1984 with a general conclusion that in order to make the field grow more efforts were needed in terms of variety of methods and a more systematic approach to empirics. The nature of his findings is not surprising as the review has more of a challenging than a systematizing character. Ten years later Gorman et al. (1997) conducted another review on entrepreneurial education based on research published between 1985 and 1994 and reported further progress in the field. The authors divided all 92 papers published in seven leading journals in entrepreneurship and small business by considering their type (empirical vs. descriptive), target market and content (with a general division into entrepreneurial propensity, pre-startup, post-startup, educational process and structure). Their overall conclusion resembles that made by Dainow (1984), as they maintain the call for a stronger empirical focus and position the field as being still in the exploratory phase. In particular, they are concerned about methodological flaws (dominance of cross-sectional surveys and measurement of variables based on self-reports, as well as a lack of theoretically derived sampling and insufficient use of existing theories). Therefore, they recommend applying a more interdisciplinary approach to research by drawing from theories developed in other disciplines, as well as encourage the use of quasi-experimental controls and more rigour in choosing and presenting the research samples.

The next decade brought two other interesting literature reviews on the progress of entrepreneurial education; a paper by Béchard and Grégoire (2005) and the study by Pittaway and Cope (2007). In their review, Béchard and Grégoire (2005) considered only articles concerning entrepreneurship education in the context of higher education. They reviewed 103 papers published between 1984 and 2002 with an aim "to document which education preoccupations animate entrepreneurship research concerned with higher education" (p. 35). They identified four dominant types of education research preoccupations: social, technological, academic and personalist ones, whereas social-cognitive, psycho-cognitive and spiritualist or ethical dimensions are underrepresented. Their view on the progress of entrepreneurial education is fairly positive; however, they note that the focus on theory development and institutional legitimacy results in scarce educational implications and also recognize the lack of educational expertise on the part of many researchers in the field. They find entrepreneurial education, which demands expertise in two fields – entrepreneurship and education – challenging and stress the need for more reference to the scholarly output in education, as otherwise the development of entrepreneurial education might be only driven by practice and remain contextual. Pittaway and Cope (2007) reviewed 185 journal papers from 1970 to 2004. Using thematic analysis and narrative coding, they searched abstracts and grouped themes related to entrepreneurial education. This mapping of the field led the authors to the conclusion that the evidence is still fragmentary. Pittaway and Cope (2007, p. 498) wrote about entrepreneurial education "the work that has been carried out tends to be conducted in isolation from other important work: in adult learning; management learning; HE policy; graduate employment; and labour markets". Therefore, the problem of separation from more developed (sub-)disciplines was raised again. Their study also calls for entrepreneurial education research to be more context related, as there is only marginal consensus on what entrepreneurship means when applied in education practice.

Heading into the next decade of the field's development, Mwasalwiba's (2010) review paper on entrepreneurship education seeks to address the broad agreement among scholars on the key content to be covered when teaching entrepreneurship and argues for experience-based pedagogy (an active approach). The paper also acknowledges that the assumption on how to teach (more actively) might not mirror classroom practice, as many of the teaching methods used reflect passive approaches (lectures, case studies and group discussions) (Mwasalwiba, 2010).

Many interesting observations and recommendations are regularly presented by Alain Fayolle. In his article from 2013 he sees the progress in entrepreneurial education as dependent on issues such as: relevance, self-consistency, usefulness, effectiveness and efficiency of teaching (Fayolle, 2013). On a research level, he observes a lack of critical thinking and approach when investigating issues related to entrepreneurial education and a problem of a potential disconnection from entrepreneurial practice. To achieve the desirable connection there is a need to build professional circles and networks. This would create a target (identifying an appropriate focus), the development of connections (both with the entrepreneurship and general education fields) and finally introspection (reflecting on the field and its progress), as recommended by Fayolle (2013). Following the call for a target, connection and introspection, Fayolle and colleagues (2016) provide a valuable synthesis of the condition of entrepreneurial education research in terms of gaining legitimacy. In their editorial paper they enumerate the following problems with entrepreneurial education as a field: insufficient conceptual and methodological foundations, remaining fragmented and descriptive, lack of clarity of the pedagogical objectives and learning outcomes as a result of the lack of agreement on the nature of the entrepreneurship phenomenon. Again, the weaknesses seem to recur. As a remedy to these problems, they suggest drawing from other disciplines (in particular education science), placing more emphasis on specific concepts and processes and advancing reflexive knowledge on the pedagogical practice and the institutional context it enables.

Another important paper drawing on the systematic review methodology is the study by Nabi et al. (2017). The authors focus on the impact of entrepreneurial education in higher education and try to deepen the understanding of the difference between methods used in the entrepreneurship classroom and their outcomes. They note that sound entrepreneurship education impact research is still marginal and even if it is examined there is a clear tendency to use only short-term, simplistic and often subjective impact indicators. The most common evaluation concentrates on entrepreneurial intentions, disregarding, for example, the development of an entrepreneurial mindset or emotions and often ignoring some contextual issue that could explain the achieved outcomes. Therefore, they call for higher-level impact indicators for evaluating entrepreneurial education, the consideration of a greater number of factors that could clarify the findings and recommend competence-model-related pedagogical methods for further exploration. When we compare the findings of Nabi et al. (2017) with the data from Chapter 3, we see that some progress has been made, as almost 30 percent of the papers in our samples qualified for the evaluation category. However, when exploring further, the studies in our sample do not correspond to the research recommendations suggested by Nabi et al. (2017) in their table, indicating the intention-to-behaviour gap, the contextual contradictions, the role of pedagogical methods for impact and measuring emotions and mindsets.

Bringing us to the present, a broad and comprehensive systematic literature review of the evolution of pedagogy in entrepreneurial education research has recently been published by Hägg and Gabrielsson (2019). They analysed 395 articles published between 1980 and 2018 in their attempt to reconstruct the evolution of the research on pedagogy in entrepreneurial education. They divide the evolution of pedagogy in entrepreneurial education into four phases corresponding to the last four decades. The first decade, the 1980s, is called a teacher-oriented period, the second, the 1990s, a process-centred period, the third, the 2000s, a context-centred period and finally the last decade a learner-centred one. In those four decades, teaching methods changed from didactic teaching methods (in the form of lectures, guest lectures and case studies) – also termed a passive approach (see Mwasalwiba, 2010) – through didactic and action-oriented teaching (business plans, lectures, guest lectures and case studies) and experiential learning (real life ventures) towards an experiential and constructivist perspective on learning (lean start-up and business model canvas). The paper gives us a panoramic view of how pedagogical methods have developed and changed in the field of entrepreneurial education.

The work of Hägg and Gabrielsson (2019) has been continued by Gabrielsson and colleagues (2020) with the aim of addressing various aspects of pedagogy in entrepreneurial education from a bibliometric methodological standpoint and by Landström and colleagues (2021) by taking stock of the social structure of entrepreneurial education as a scientific field. The study by Gabrielsson et al. (2020) had a particular interest in changes in the core topics and scholarly work between 1995 and 2018. Their analysis confirmed a significant increase in the number of scholars and articles in the field of entrepreneurial education and also demonstrated a growing diversification of the research output built on the basis of an expanding knowledge base (measured by the number of references). However, according to their research, the later years (2013–2018) resulted in a more homogeneous and interconnected knowledge base, which might be interpreted as the maturation of the field and its research grounding. Moving to the present, the study by Landström et al. (2021) pays particular attention to the scholarly community and how key journals, conferences and influential authors have come to shape the communities. In their study they find four communities that do not appear to have many scholarly connections, which leads them to critically question the small core community of entrepreneurial education scholars that seems to drive the field forward. In their concluding argument they see a vulnerability in the loose connections between the different communities and that the core community is becoming more research oriented, which might impede the practice-oriented characteristics that created interest in the field in the first place (as acknowledged by Hägg and Gabrielsson, 2019). Finally, Landström et al. (2021) position entrepreneurial education as a "socially-based scholarly field" where the importance of keeping the field together can be achieved by the development of communication systems (e.g., journals and meeting places), thus enabling entrepreneurial education to survive and thrive as a scholarly field.

4.2 Challenges of Entrepreneurial Education Research

Summarizing the above reviews on the development of entrepreneurial education research and the empirical insights derived from Chapter 3, there seem to be three main challenges that require continuous verification:

1. The challenge of more theory-oriented research,
2. The challenge of a methodical and rigorous approach to conducting research to achieve an accumulation of knowledge in entrepreneurial education,
3. The challenge of presenting a clear-cut context (both cultural and learning) through which research findings are interpreted but with a view to creating shared frameworks for the field.

In an attempt to respond to these continuous calls for action we will address these challenges taking into consideration the two questions posed in the introduction that have guided our empirical analysis as well as the findings from the above-mentioned reviews.

4.2.1 The Challenge of More Theory-Oriented Research

Starting with the challenge of more theory-oriented research, our results clearly show that the frequency of publishing theory-driven papers is increasing over time, as illustrated in Figure 3.11 in Chapter 3 of this book. A positive fact is that in the last decade, theory-driven papers, i.e., papers with clear theory development, accounted for about 43 percent of all papers published during this period. The increasing trend of contributing to the theory of entrepreneurial education is also enhanced by the eclectic theory papers, which accounted for about 16 percent. However, it is very difficult to objectively assess whether these numbers are high enough and what is the norm. Despite a downward trend in the number of atheoretical papers or ones without an explicit theory, it is alarming that they still constitute about 41 percent of all papers published since 2010. It goes without saying that we should bear in mind the still relatively short lifetime of the field and as a result collaboration between entrepreneurial education scholars is only starting to emerge, the small number of researchers with a degree in entrepreneurial education continue their research efforts within the field, and the high dependency on the advancement of entrepreneurship research. The research community has only recently strengthened its position, proof of which is entrepreneurial education focused conferences (such as 3E or USASBE) or the European Entrepreneurship Education Award. Nevertheless, despite the obvious progress in terms of theoretical approach in the examined papers, the need for more theory advancement in the field must be voiced once again in this book, similar to the claim made by most of the researchers we referred to earlier. We are on the right track when it comes to development, but still more consensus on a common understanding of basic concepts, which constitutes the starting point for theory development, is needed for more research legitimacy. The probability of achieving this consensus is increasing with cross-institution, cross-country and cross-continental cooperation of academics. Following the trends of this cooperation (Figures 3.3– 3.5 in Chapter 3), it becomes evident that greater efforts are required to enhance the dialogue between researchers of different backgrounds and teaching experience in order to build a common ground for future studies. More intense theoretical advancement would perhaps naturalize and meet the continuous call for publication in higher ranked journals, which in turn increases credibility and visibility on the research map. It should be noted that the perspectives are promising if we take into consideration the emergence of *Entrepreneurship Education and Pedagogy* in 2018, the first journal entirely devoted to entrepreneurial education with high ambitions in terms of its position on the publishing market. In addition, an increasing number of special issues entirely dedicated to entrepreneurial education in well-established international journals, such as the *Journal of Small Business Management* in 2019 or the *International Journal of Entrepreneurial Behaviour & Research* in 2020 means that the field is growing and will consolidate its position in the coming years.

4.2.2 The Challenge of a Methodological and Rigorous Approach to Conducting Research

The second outlined challenge concerns a methodical and rigorous approach to conducting research to achieve an accumulation of knowledge in entrepreneurial education. While the rigour of writing is difficult to assess, progress has been made in terms of methodical approach. Addressing the concerns brought up by Gorman et al. (1997) as well as in other prominent studies such as Pittaway and Cope (2007), Fayolle (2013) and Rideout and Gray (2013), there seems to be scholarly progress that finally starts to meet the call for action that has been made continuously over the last four decades. However, as the field is broad and comprises different viewpoints and scholarly backgrounds, which was evident in the study by Landström et al. (2021), where a majority of scholars have a business background followed by those with degrees in education and pedagogy, the methodological harmony that we address in Chapter 3 mirrors the diversity of scholars. Given that much pedagogical and educational research focuses on the experiences undertaken by students in the classroom setting or beyond it, the amount of qualitative empirical work is to be expected. However, the balance of quantitative studies also brings up the legacy of management research and the more positivistic tradition that can be found in mainstream entrepreneurship research (see Landström, Harirchic, & Åström, 2012). Although claims for legitimacy and the movement towards rigour in scholarly studies are called for (Fayolle et al., 2016; Rideout & Gray, 2013), there is a fine balance to strike between overly academic discussions that merely consider the scientific sophistication in the use of methods and relevance to practice. Because entrepreneurial education as a field of research has a profound practice orientation and the scholarly discussion is close to reality, we should not forget that progress might differ from that in less practice-based fields. In our analysis we see progress and increased sophistication in the use of a broad variety of methods, both qualitative and quantitative, but a major challenge still persists. This challenge is the need for more pre- and post-studies as well as longitudinal studies that could capture the so often sought behavioural patterns to justify the different learning activities and learning theories that are championed by the various scholars in the field. We are still not seeing a progressive increase in longitudinal studies that could capture these behavioural changes, and the question of what we actually measure when we measure outcomes still remains. In addition, the argument made by Gorman et al. (1997) for more quasi-experimental controls in entrepreneurial education is still valid and has not been largely adopted to create more rigour in the stated outcomes of studies in the field. Hence, a key question that still remains unanswered concerns rigour in measuring behavioural change as well as the need for experimental controls. However, we are not claiming to have a clear-cut answer for what to actually measure, but a claim that can be made is to rethink the short-term timespans that only investigate short courses or a couple of educational interventions, as they are unlikely to capture the behavioural change.

4.2.3   The Challenge of Presenting a Clear-Cut Context

The third challenge outlined relates to adequately presenting the context through which research findings are interpreted. However, a context influences not only the way data are viewed and depicted but the whole research process, from formulating assumptions, posing research questions or stating hypothesis to the description of observations and their analysis. As stated in Chapter 2, context plays a significant role in the field of entrepreneurial education due to the fact that it has now become a global phenomenon and the diversity of meaning that being entrepreneurial has come to illustrate. The results of our study strengthen this claim, as the meaning of context is particularly important when considering the weak international or even cross-institution collaboration between researchers and the fact that almost 30 percent of the papers published in the investigated period were written by single authors. There is, however, a more pressing issue than the single author dilemma that can be seen in the sample. It concerns the slow development of and lack of progress in cross-continental collaboration that could create more harmony between different views on what entrepreneurship or enterprising might mean and how the different viewpoints could cross-fertilize to strengthen the field as a whole. One reason for the narrowness of context might be due to the difficulties of multidisciplinary expertise as argued by Béchard and Grégoire (2005), who stated that the field demands expertise in both entrepreneurship and education. Given the development seen in Chapter 3, the field seems to be driven by a practice agenda and the contextual setting of the studies remains fairly local, hence we are still not seeing a broad alignment and progression of multi-contextual studies that could decrease this call for action. More international research teams would enable break from the routinized analytical patterns of studying one's own classroom setting and provide opportunities for theoretical and methodological validations as claimed by past scholarly works (Bechard & Toulouse, 1998; Nabi et al., 2017; Rideout & Gray, 2013). The issue of contextual confusion or rather contextual barriers is also present in the study by Landström et al. (2021) regarding their findings that the field includes four distinct communities. They argue that there is a great need to unite these communities and build a global community that despite local or national differences could both aggregate and harmonize some fundamental common grounds that create boundary conditions for what entrepreneurial education might mean. Nor do we see any response to the critical call made by Pittaway and Cope (2007) that there is only marginal consensus on what entrepreneurship means when applied in education practice, which might also be connected to the diversity of the meaning applied to the phenomenon in different contexts around the globe. The meaning or boundary condition was also highlighted by Hytti and O'Gorman (2004), who argued for more conceptual clarity due to the blurred understanding of the terms entrepreneurship and enterprise. However, there is still much inconclusiveness despite many similarities that could have been further advanced through more collaborative work as seen in our analysis and the continuous call for clarity in the various reviews that we have addressed in this chapter. From a perspective spanning almost four decades, there has been a significant increase in entrepreneurial education literature. In addition, more complex research designs and advanced methods and techniques have been applied and the general trend involves not only describing what works in entrepreneurial education but also explaining some causalities. Guided by a practice-oriented research agenda, the field has made its presence known on the scientific map but considerable work still remains to earn a more long-term chair in the academic community.

4.3 The Specifics of Entrepreneurial Education Research

Discovering the specific features of entrepreneurial education as a research field requires indicating both its strengths and weaknesses. The characteristics mentioned here are based on the findings from Chapters 1–3, including our empirical study, as well as the result of the synthesis of the aforementioned literature reviews.

Major weaknesses of entrepreneurial education research:

- *Strong ties with economic policy.* They initially helped to build the foundations of the field and its overall recognition, but have since hindered its academic identity among other research disciplines due to the fact that the research on entrepreneurial education developed more slowly than the practice of its education.
- *A strong identification with neoliberalism.* This in turn is associated with fast-growing, competitive firms and the enterprising self-ideal, which began to attract criticism due to the high pressure to achieve profits leading to a competitive race among citizens and growing inequalities in society.
- *Dependency on the advancement of two other research fields: entrepreneurship and general education.* This made entrepreneurial

education unique, but at the same time its development requires the monitoring of scientific progress in two related fields that has created a heightened complexity for scholars migrating into the field.

- *The profile of researchers in the field.* First of all, there is often a potential bias if the teacher is also conducting studies on her/his own methods and students. In addition, there are still not many researchers who have completed their doctoral studies in entrepreneurial education and continue to conduct the research within the field. If they exist, they work individually rather than creating bigger research centres (with only a few exceptions).

- *An uneven geographical distribution of researchers and consequently unbalanced entrepreneurial contexts of studies.* There is a clear dominance of the US, the UK, Canada and the Scandinavian countries when learning and teaching environments are described, which may lead to a skewed picture of what entrepreneurial education looks like.

- *Relatively weak collaboration between entrepreneurial education researchers from different institutions,* in particular from different countries or continents, creating sub-communities and internal tribalism that could lead to reduced consolidation on where the field is heading and inability to reach consensus on key characteristics that could enable scholars to build the field despite internal differences.

- *A selective view on learning* where the focus in research is placed on the contents and method (what and how to learn), whereas the learning process, the learners and their abilities or entry-level characteristics for learning receive far less attention.

- *A problem with generalization of research findings* as a result of the multitude and broadness of contexts (in terms of learning environments as well as cultural environments).

- *The problem of a balance between exploratory and explicative research.* The former concerns the search for new knowledge, inspiring new theories, concepts and explanations. The latter concerns the application and development of the existing research output. Exploratory research contributes to the construction of science, while explicative research integrates and validates the existing knowledge base. The exploratory approach has so far dominated in entrepreneurial education. This raises another major problem for entrepreneurial education as a research field – the problem of replication. Replicating research in entrepreneurial education is difficult, but necessary to confirm or reject hypotheses.

Major strengths of entrepreneurial education research:

- *An image of entrepreneurial education as a progressive field contributing to societal and economic development,* supporting the importance of conducting research in this academic subject. The progressiveness is also flexible towards the surrounding trends related to the world of work and should be pointed out as a strength to merit a place in academia to educate the future work force.
- *An interest in the research on entrepreneurial education as a result of the growth of the start-up culture.* Despite the fact that neoliberal and enterprising self ideals are somewhat negatively viewed in society, the importance of equipping individuals with entrepreneurial skills and abilities will most likely increase in the future, which positions entrepreneurial education as an important vehicle.
- *Highly applicative character of the discipline.* The close ties of the research in entrepreneurial education to both teaching and practicing entrepreneurship enable quick verification of its results.
- *Strong practical implications of the research findings.* The strong practical implications that emerge from research in entrepreneurial education are dependent on maintaining a good balance between rigour and relevance and keeping the practice-based approach that reduces the risk of the field becoming overly academic in its scope, where refinements of measurement would decrease the potential to communicate for the benefit of societal stakeholders. Although this balance is good, it is also a barrier to achieving publication in high-impact journals and perhaps a trade-off needs to be further discussed.
- *The rise in the number of research publications in the area of entrepreneurial education,* which goes hand in hand with the theoretical and methodological advancement.
- *The growing community of researchers in entrepreneurial education* and increasing formal organization of science. The number of research units/centres dealing with this research domain, the number of doctors and professors in the field and the number of journals, publications, monographs and conferences devoted to entrepreneurial education is increasing.

- *The growth of the "internal" citation rate in the field of entrepreneurial education* – researchers refer to more and more scientific achievements in the field of entrepreneurial education, not only related sciences, and thus the strength and distinctiveness of the field is growing. This is an important development that can decrease the heterogeneity and may lead to some aggregate boundary conditions that could define the field and create a more stable arena in the academic landscape.
- *The recent emergence of critical studies* on entrepreneurial education as an academic subject, which is regarded as a sign of maturity of the field. Although critical studies are needed and following the call from Fayolle and colleagues (2016) there is a need for introspection, it is at the same time a bit tricky to point out what is actually being critiqued, as the boundary conditions have yet to fully emerge. However, an inward-looking scrutiny is useful to further the field in its development.

As the research advances, entrepreneurial education continuously identifies areas of interest and defines their boundaries and further directions for development. However, there are still no strictly defined basic terms and concepts, and researchers do not use a coherent conceptual apparatus or a specific methodology and scientific rigour. The lack of a theory of entrepreneurial education is compensated for by a set of multi- and interdisciplinary approaches that do not always use the same conceptual frame. This is at odds with the orthodox approach to research, assuming the existence of verifiable theories and the consistent use of a scientific method. It can therefore be concluded that entrepreneurial education still aspires to be a fully independent research field as it has not yet developed all the structures typical of autonomous discipline. Drawing from many fields is typical for the crystallization phase of a new discipline and typical for ones developed in times of atomization of science. Entrepreneurial education as a research field should try to objectify and generalize the results.

4.4 Future of Entrepreneurial Education as a Research Field

The above discussion allows us to determine the overall future research agenda – the recommended directions of research efforts leading to the development of the entrepreneurial education field. We divided them into three areas: thematic, methodological and research collaboration, as illustrated in Table 4.1.

Table 4.1 Recommendation for the future research agenda

Themes

- Merging the insights about practicing entrepreneurs with the knowledge already developed in the field of education in order to understand how the systematic process of education generates fruitful learning for students who undertake education in entrepreneurship
- Decomposing and recreating the entrepreneurial learning process, leading to knowledge generation in entrepreneurship
- Understanding differences in students' learning of entrepreneurship and their consequences for teaching practice
- Following the dynamics of experiential learning, including action orientation and reflective practice; exploring transformation of experience and its empowering role in learning
- Examining the role and meaning of the cultural and institutional contexts of learning and teaching
- Developing the perspective of a learner as a recipient of entrepreneurial education and learner-centred entrepreneurial education
- Referring to developmental psychology in order to understand the cognitive capabilities of learners and their learning profiles, thus in addition to *what* and *how* to teach, *who* are the recipients of educational interventions and challenging the actual match between the maturity of learners and the methods used are also important
- Developing a critical approach to the methods in entrepreneurial education
- Measuring the effectiveness of methods in entrepreneurial education and evaluating teaching practices
- Following the influence of social and economic trends, such as the sharing economy, the circular economy, the gig economy, or the postgrowth economy, on entrepreneurship and entrepreneurial education
- Developing characteristics of entrepreneurial education as a progressive movement

Methods

- Seeking specific methods of conducting research in entrepreneurial education
- Going beyond descriptive analysis of the empirics
- Increasing and diversifying samples
- More focus on longitudinal studies
- Replicating the most meaningful research in entrepreneurial education and contextualizing the results
- Viewing entrepreneurial education in the context of the development of entrepreneurship research that addresses the contextual difference of sub-disciplines in entrepreneurship

(continued)

Table 4.1 Cont.

Collaboration

- Forming research groups with researchers beyond the same research circle, institution and country
- Building research groups where entrepreneurship teachers/instructors are not the only ones to interpret data when the research context relates to their programme, course or students
- Collaborating for the introduction of more special issues related to entrepreneurial education and publication in more recognized journals
- Promoting the entrepreneurial education field through, for example, creating new book series devoted to the field and continuing the special awards, similar to the European Entrepreneurship Education Award, as well as special events at conferences such as the 3E or USASBE
- Continuing the integration of the community of entrepreneurial education scholars, but with "gatekeepers" to protect the quality of the research
- Addressing the emerging divergence between some sub-fields of entrepreneurial education research (such as engineering entrepreneurial education) and more mainstream entrepreneurship education research

---

References

Béchard, J.-P., & Grégoire, D. (2005). Entrepreneurship education research revisited: the case of higher education. *Academy of Management Learning & Education, 4*(1), 22–43.

Bechard, J.-P., & Toulouse, J.-M. (1998). Validation of a didactic model for the analysis of training objectives in entrepreneurship. *Journal of Business Venturing, 13*(4), 317–332.

Béchard, J.-P., & Toulouse, J.-M. (1991). Entrepreneurship and education: viewpoint from education. *Journal of Small Business & Entrepreneurship, 9*(1), 3–13.

Dainow, R. (1986). Training and education of entrepreneurs: the current state of the literature. *Journal of Small Business & Entrepreneurship, 3*(4), 10–23.

Fayolle, A. (2013). Personal views on the future of entrepreneurship education. *Entrepreneurship & Regional Development, 25*(7-8), 692–701.

Fayolle, A., Verzat, C., & Wapshott, R. (2016). In quest of legitimacy: the theoretical and methodological foundations of entrepreneurship education research. *International Small Business Journal, 34*(7), 895–904.

Gabrielsson, J., Hägg, G., Landström, H., & Politis, D. (2020). Connecting the past with the present: the development of research on pedagogy in entrepreneurial education. *Education + Training, 62*(9), 1061–1086.

Gorman, G., Hanlon, D., & King, W. (1997). Some research perspectives on entrepreneurship education, enterprise education and education for small business management: a ten-year literature review. *International Small Business Journal, 15*(3), 56–77.

Hägg, G., & Gabrielsson, J. (2019). A systematic literature review of the evolution of pedagogy in entrepreneurial education research. *International Journal of Entrepreneurial Behavior & Research, 26*(5), 829–861.

Hytti, U., & O'Gorman, C. (2004). What is 'enterprise education'? An analysis of the objectives and methods of enterprise education programmes in four European countries. *Education + Training, 46*(1), 11–23.Kyrö, P. (2015). The conceptual contribution of education to research on entrepreneurship education. *Entrepreneurship & Regional Development, 27*(9–10), 599–618.

Landström, H., Harirchic, G., & Åström, F. (2012). Entrepreneurship: exploring the knowledge base. *Research Policy, 41*, 1154–1181.

Landström, H., Gabrielsson, J., Politis, D., Sörheim, R., & Djupdal, K. (2021). The social structure of entrepreneurial education as a scientific field. *Academy of Management Learning & Education.* doi:https://doi.org/10.5465/amle.2020.0140

Mwasalwiba, E. S. (2010). Entrepreneurship education: a review of its objectives, teaching methods, and impact indicators. *Education + Training, 52*(1), 20–47.

Nabi, G., Liñán, F., Fayolle, A., Krueger, N., & Walmsley, A. (2017). The impact of entrepreneurship education in higher education: a systematic review and research agenda. *Academy of Management Learning & Education, 16*(2), 277–299.

Pittaway, L., & Cope, J. (2007). Entrepreneurship education a systematic review of the evidence. *International Small Business Journal, 25*(5), 479–510.

Rideout, E. C., & Gray, D. O. (2013). Does entrepreneurship education really work? A review and methodological critique of the empirical literature on the effects of university-based entrepreneurship education. *Journal of Small Business Management, 51*(3), 329–351.

Sexton, D. L., & Bowman, N. B. (1984). Entrepreneurship education: suggestions for increasing effectiveness. *Journal of Small Business Management, 22*(2), 18–25.

Sexton, D. L., & Bowman-Upton, N. (1987). Evaluation of an innovative approach to teaching entrepreneurship. *Journal of Small Business Management, 25*(1), 35–43.

Conclusion
Scholarly Progress and Future Challenges

Throughout the development of the book, we have strived to maintain a balanced and integrative tone that does not focus on individual level differences between the narrow and the broad conceptualization of entrepreneurial education. In this concluding chapter, we return to the initial discussion that has motivated the book, the idea of a balance between rigour and relevance, as well as the evolutionary discussion on what entrepreneurship or enterprising or entrepreneurial education might actually mean. Hence, the following section will discuss the scholarly progress that has been achieved and end with deliberations on future challenges or the call for action to create wholeness for harmonizing the development of the field.

C.1 How to Balance Rigour and Relevance in Entrepreneurial Education Research

Over the last four decades the field of entrepreneurial education, including entrepreneurship and enterprising education, has seen a remarkable progression from being a policy tool during the early days to stimulate the growth of start-ups and small businesses towards becoming a worldwide (although viewed as heterogeneous) community (Hägg & Gabrielsson, 2019; Landström, Gabrielsson, Politis, Sörheim, & Djupdal, 2021) where courses and programmes can be found in basically all different faculties (Morris & Liguori, 2016). Given the discussion and empirical analysis brought forward in this book, there are some clear conclusions regarding scholarly progress. We can infer from the analysis and additional literature reviews of the field that there is both theoretical development and methodological refinement.

The theoretical progress is particularly visible if we retrospectively examine the development of the field throughout the last four decades. The proportion of papers with sound theorizing is increasing with time,

DOI: 10.4324/9781003194972-5

which leads to slow but continuous development in entrepreneurial education as a research-driven discipline with full academic legitimacy. In particular, the growing interest in experience-based learning and action learning is noted and these concepts are regularly translated into entrepreneurial education theoretical frameworks. More intense theorizing goes hand in hand with the maturation of the methods applied, both qualitative and quantitative in nature. Again, the development cannot be labelled dynamic, but from the 40-year perspective, the contribution is clear in terms of the methods used, size of samples, diversification of cases and addressing the meaning of geographical and learning contexts. The advancement of both theoretical and empirical levels may be related to the quite slow yet visible positive trend of increased research collaboration between academics representing different institutions, countries and continents, which, if more common and intensified, may lead to greater integration and harmony in the field. The increased breadth and scope of entrepreneurial education with a multitude of local contexts within the field due to constant verification and the cumulative effect is currently facing the stage when a more aggregated level of knowledge is expected, while still maintaining scholarly rigour and relevance.

Furthermore, we can acknowledge that certain journal outlets have become key forums for scholarly discussion. It is especially noted that an evolving arena is materializing in *Education + Training*, which has created a stable platform for spurring a continuing discussion since the inaugural special issue was launched in 2000. But we can also see a potential new forum through the development of the *Entrepreneurship Education & Pedagogy* journal, which has provided the much-needed space both for research and more practical learning innovations. Through the dual aim of the new journal there is a continuous strive for balancing rigour and relevance, where research is becoming more theory driven with higher demands for methodological rigour, whilst simultaneously the practical relevance of what is being taught and how it is being taught is given a space for scholarly development. Hence, when analysing the articles now being published, it appears that the somewhat critical calls for more rigour to create legitimacy as a scholarly field of research are finally being answered. However, the response to the call for high-impact journal publications is still fairly low and there is little evidence indicating that scholars are targeting and being accepted by high-impact journals, which is in line with the arguments made by Landström et al. (2021) as well as by Gabrielsson, Hägg, Landström and Politis (2020). Instead, the multidisciplinary and multi-terminology that are tied to the field of entrepreneurial education research seem to have forced the field into finding own arenas where scholars can exchange ideas and maintain a vibrant academic discussion. But, as Landström et al. (2021) argue, there seems to be low consolidation across scholarly communities, which agrees with our main argument on the low continental collaboration that might decrease the aggregate understanding of the phenomenon being addressed.

Despite four decades of scholarly progress with refined theoretical development, more robust techniques for empirical analysis, use of multiple data sources and a good balance between quantitative and qualitative methods, the sub-communities and local anchoring of what entrepreneurship or enterprising might mean still obfuscate the more aggregate and global progress of the field. Although we do not claim to have a clear-cut answer, in the next section we will try to present an argument that could reduce the tribalism that might be unconsciously hindering the continental collaboration that we see as the main future challenge in developing the field as a whole.

C.2   Creating Wholeness through Entrepreneurial Education

In the education field it is argued that knowledge is never static but continuously evolving. We even went as far as arguing that we would not talk about knowledge as such but instead address it as knowing. Through the verb of knowing we are constantly in mutating from one stage to another. The ideas of not being static and talking about knowing come from John Dewey, as well as from Charles Sander Peirce and the discussion of what pragmatism implies. The main connection here is the strong adherence to pragmatism and experiential learning when talking about entrepreneurship or enterprising education. However, a main difference is that we continuously discuss these intertwined sub-fields separately, whilst the notion of entrepreneurial education might better align with the basic assumptions on learning from and through experience. A general assumption that is taken for granted in both sub-fields is found in the experiential nature of how to develop students into becoming entrepreneurs or enterprising individuals (Hägg & Kurczewska, 2020; Jones & Iredale, 2010; Jones, 2009; Neck & Corbett, 2018). There is also a general idea that entrepreneurship and enterprising education is seeking to develop students' mindsets and teach them how to handle uncertainty and become creative problem solvers (Brodie, Laing, & Anderson, 2009; Daniel, 2016; Kirby & Mullen, 1990; Laalo & Heinonen, 2016), which aspires towards the achievement of similar goals. In particular, the idea of how to become more adaptable and handle uncertainty is something that aligns. We might start to talk about a more aggregate goal of developing entrepreneurial graduates where internal differences can co-exist in whether the graduates become the narrow high growth entrepreneur or the potential change agent who is often associated with the enterprising persona (Ball, 1989). Regardless of what the final destination becomes for the entrepreneurial graduate, the idea of an aggregate construct where we talk about entrepreneurial education rhymes well with the evolving view of knowing on which our assumptions about learning and education rest. However, the transformation from knowledge to knowing or entrepreneurship/enterprising to entrepreneurial also find support in the arguments on wholeness addressed by Palmer (1998) in his book *The Courage to Teach*.

Palmer's (1998) idea of wholeness fits neatly into the prevailing crossroad discussion in entrepreneurship and enterprising education as it seeks to consolidate and create a common ground for how to strengthen polar positions instead of intensifying the critique of each side. Over the past four decades there has been a vibrant tribalism in the scholarly field that up to now has spurred outsiders, making them step into the field and contribute. However, in a relatively young field (as acknowledged in Landström et al., 2021) tribalism can also weaken the development as little consolidation occurs to create a good scholarly foundation for newcomers to lean on. Hence, we have seen over the four decades that much progress is being made in terms of the increase of theory-driven and rigorous use of methods in studies, but there are still tribal claims voiced for each side of enterprising or entrepreneurship. For example, Neck and Corbett (2018) concluded that when addressing entrepreneurship education the main starting point is the venture creation process, whilst Jones and Iredale (2010) claim that enterprising education is the transformative process and Jones and Penaluna (2013) argue for a shift from the subject-centredness of entrepreneurship to become an enterprising individual. However, these protectionist tribal arguments have in some ways created a void that Erkkilä (2000) sought to remedy at an early stage. But, in hindsight, perhaps the two fields and the scholars who moved in did not possess an absorptive capacity for the aggregate conceptualization of entrepreneurial education at that point in time. The idea of merging two fields that have sprung from a very similar foundation can be seen in the early discussions by Gibb (1987) from a UK perspective and by Ronstadt (1985) from a US perspective, which has much merit in terms of consolidating the scholarly knowledge developed in each sub-domain. Perhaps the field is more open for this potential consolidation or wholeness as Palmer (1998) terms it. Wholeness is explained as the connecting nodes of a battery, where one needs both the positive and the negative poles in order to generate power. If one uses only the negative or the positive pole, no power will be found. Hence, we should talk about entrepreneurship insights *and* enterprising insights making up the wholeness of entrepreneurial insights. It is only by connecting the two that we can discuss how to further the field and create wholeness among the apparent tribes or as Landström et al. (2021) describe them, different communities that have rather weak ties.

Wholeness is a good reminder that polarization might not be the solution for future progression (Palmer, 1998). Instead by creating an aggregate umbrella terminology such as the use of entrepreneurial education, which includes insights from entrepreneurship as a narrower approach as well as from enterprising as a broader approach, the tribalism that seems to have emerged due to little agreement on the phenomenon could perhaps be reduced. We are not arguing against the differences that create the dynamism needed to challenge established and sometimes taken-for-granted assumptions, but rather seeking consolidation to create space for the much-needed international and cross-continental collaboration, which is one of the main challenges found in our study.

References

Ball, C. (1989). *Towards an 'enterprising' culture: a challenge for education and training.* (4). Paris, France: OECD/CERI.

Brodie, J., Laing, S., & Anderson, M. (2009). Developing enterprising people through an innovative enterprise degree: an analysis of the students' evolving perceptions and attitudes. *Industry and Higher Education, 23*(3), 233–241.

Daniel, A. D. (2016). Fostering an entrepreneurial mindset by using a design thinking approach in entrepreneurship education. *Industry and Higher Education, 30*(3), 215–223.

Erkkilä, K. (2000). *Entrepreneurial education: mapping the debates in the United States, the United Kingdom and Finland.* London: Garland, Taylor & Francis.

Gabrielsson, J., Hägg, G., Landström, H., & Politis, D. (2020). Connecting the past with the present: the development of research on pedagogy in entrepreneurial education. *Education + Training, 62*(9), 1061–1086.

Gibb, A. A. (1987). Enterprise culture – its meaning and implications for education and training. *Journal of European Industrial Training, 11*(2), 2–38.

Hägg, G., & Gabrielsson, J. (2019). A systematic literature review of the evolution of pedagogy in entrepreneurial education research. *International Journal of Entrepreneurial Behavior & Research, 26*(5), 829–861.

Hägg, G., & Kurczewska, A. (2020). Towards a learning philosophy based on experience in entrepreneurship education. *Entrepreneurship Education & Pedagogy, 3*(2), 129–153.

Jones, B., & Iredale, N. (2010). Enterprise education as pedagogy. *Education + Training, 52*(1), 7–19.

Jones, C. (2009). Enterprise education: learning through personal experience. *Industry and Higher Education, 23*(3), 175–182.

Jones, C., & Penaluna, A. (2013). Moving beyond the business plan in enterprise education. *Education + Training, 55*(8/9), 804–814.

Kirby, D. A., & Mullen, D. (1990). Developing enterprising graduates. *Journal of European Industrial Training, 14*(2), 27–32.

Laalo, H., & Heinonen, J. (2016). Governing the entrepreneurial mindset: Business students' constructions of entrepreneurial subjectivity. *European Educational Research Journal, 15*(6), 696–713.

Landström, H., Gabrielsson, J., Politis, D., Sörheim, R., & Djupdal, K. (2021). The social structure of entrepreneurial education as a scientific field. *Academy of Management Learning & Education*. doi:https://doi.org/10.5465/amle.2020.0140

Morris, M. H., & Liguori, E. (2016). *Annals of Entrepreneurship Education and Pedagogy–2016*. Cheltenham, UK: Edward Elgar.

Neck, H. M., & Corbett, A. C. (2018). The scholarship of teaching and learning entrepreneurship. *Entrepreneurship Education & Pedagogy, 1*(1), 8–41.

Palmer, P. (1998). *The courage to teach: exploring the inner landscape of a teacher's life*. San Francisco, CA: Jossey-Bass.

Ronstadt, R. (1985). The educated entrepreneurs: a new era of entrepreneurial education is beginning. *American Journal of Small Business, 10*(1), 7–23.

Index